Walk in
Faith

Publications International, Ltd.

Photography from Shutterstock.com

Scripture quotations are taken from the *King James Version*
of the Bible.
Additional scripture quotations are taken from the *New King
James Version®*. Copyright © 1982 by Thomas Nelson, Inc. Used by
permission. All rights reserved.

Author: Marie D. Jones

Louis Weber, CEO
Publications International, Ltd.
8140 Lehigh Avenue
Morton Grove, IL 60053

Permission is never granted for commercial purposes.

ISBN: 978-1-68022-872-4

Manufactured in China.

8 7 6 5 4 3 2 1

January

January 1

Lord, who shall abide in thy tabernacle? who shall dwell in thy holy hill? He that walketh uprightly, and worketh righteousness, and speaketh the truth in his heart. He that backbiteth not with his tongue, nor doeth evil to his neighbour, nor taketh up a reproach against his neighbour.

Psalm 15:1–3

Our strengths were given to us to help us serve. God rejoices when we change our "How can I help myself?" attitude to one of "How can I help others?" A dedicated servant is grateful to all those who have served him, including the Lord. He sees that he is passing on to others what he has received.

January 2

Thus saith the LORD, What iniquity have your fathers found in me, that they are gone far from me, and have walked after vanity, and are become vain?

Jeremiah 2:5

God doesn't only want our words of faith. He wants us to walk our talk and put our faith into everything we do. God doesn't want just prayers. He wants follow-up on our end to show we are partners with him, trusting his will as we go along. God doesn't want simple proclamations. He wants actions that show we are listening to his guidance and following his direction.

January 3

My son, walk not thou in the way with them; refrain thy foot from their path: For their feet run to evil, and make haste to shed blood.

Proverbs 1:15–16

The power of forgiveness comes from having a deep faith that God will take care of those we must part from. Maybe they caused us harm. God will deal with them. Maybe they betrayed us. God will show them the light. Having faith in God means we can forgive and move on, but only when we let him work things out on our behalf.

January 4

And all the nations shall be gathered unto it, to the name of the LORD, to Jerusalem: neither shall they walk any more after the imagination of their evil heart.

Jeremiah 3:17

So much of the crippling weight we carry upon our shoulders can be alleviated by simply understanding that we don't have to carry the burden alone. God is always there, walking beside us, and ready to take the entire load from us should we only ask him to. All of God's followers are unified by their faith in his protection.

January 5

For the LORD God is a sun and shield: the LORD will give grace and glory: no good thing will he withhold from them that walk uprightly.

Psalm 84:11

Having God in your life is like having a constant companion and best friend that is always looking out for you, and always has your back. Faith in the eternal promise of God's love is better than any superpower, because it really can bring blessings and miracles to you at any time, and you don't even need a cape.

January 6

*Noah was a just man and perfect in his generations,
and Noah walked with God.*

Genesis 6:9

At the dawn of creation, God laid out his plans for the universe, and the plan is still working. Our days are only worth living when the Lord is the director of them. When did you last pause to recognize God's wisdom in the timing of events in your life? Have you thanked him?

January 7

But the children of Israel walked upon dry land in the midst of the sea; and the waters were a wall unto them on their right hand, and on their left.

Exodus 14:29

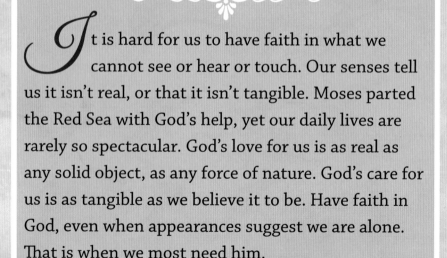

It is hard for us to have faith in what we cannot see or hear or touch. Our senses tell us it isn't real, or that it isn't tangible. Moses parted the Red Sea with God's help, yet our daily lives are rarely so spectacular. God's love for us is as real as any solid object, as any force of nature. God's care for us is as tangible as we believe it to be. Have faith in God, even when appearances suggest we are alone. That is when we most need him.

January 8

When the unclean spirit is gone out of a man, he walketh through dry places, seeking rest, and findeth none.

Matthew 12:43

When I have one foot in the worldly scene and one foot in your kingdom, Lord, I'm compromising. Your ways of humility, love, and forgiveness are so at odds with worldly material values that there is no way to play both fields at once. I have a choice to make. Do I choose to indulge in a lifetime of hedonistic pleasures, or will I choose to serve you, walking in your peaceful ways now and looking forward to the promise of eternity? I know what I choose, Lord. That's why I'm spending time with you right now. Help me to walk without compromise today.

January 9

For the LORD giveth wisdom: out of his mouth cometh knowledge and understanding. He layeth up sound wisdom for the righteous: he is a buckler to them that walk uprightly.

Proverbs 2:6–7

It's one thing to put our faith in God, but another thing entirely to let him take control. We often want to continue to hold onto our problems and complaints, thinking we can do a better job of fixing them, even when attempts have proven otherwise. Only when we truly let it all go and turn it all over can we see that our faith was well-placed from the start.

January 10

Thus saith the LORD, Stand ye in the ways, and see, and ask for the old paths, where is the good way, and walk therein, and ye shall find rest for your souls.

Jeremiah 6:16

*L*ook to God for all things, and put your faith in him. When you don't know whether to go right or left, ask God, and then do what he instructs you to do. When you can't see right from wrong, turn within, and then follow the directions you receive. God is at your service 24/7, but you have to be the one to follow through in thoughts, words, and deeds.

January 11

Yea, though I walk through the valley of the shadow of death, I will fear no evil: for thou art with me; thy rod and thy staff they comfort me.

Psalm 23:4

Guide my steps today so that I might help others and be a light in the world, especially for those who are weak and troubled. I pray for the courage to stand against injustices and to reach out to my fellow humans without fear or concern of the repercussions. I am ready to be a force for good, Lord. I am willing to step into a purpose that is founded in love and in spreading that love to all I meet. All I ask is that you direct my actions and keep me strong and pure in spirit. Amen.

January 12

Hearken now unto my voice, I will give thee counsel, and God shall be with thee: Be thou for the people to God-ward, that thou mayest bring the causes unto God: And thou shalt teach them ordinances and laws, and shalt shew them the way wherein they must walk, and the work that they must do.

Exodus 18:19

Wherever you go, wherever you look, wherever you travel, wherever you tread—whether to the left or to the right, whether up to the sky or down to the sea—God is already there, waiting for you to arrive. In all situations, let us express our gratitude to God.

January 13

Wilt thou not revive us again: that thy people may rejoice in thee?
Shew us thy mercy, O LORD, and grant us thy salvation.

Psalm 85:6–7

As we receive God's mercy, we bless others with it. God's spirit inspires good deeds that bring help to those in need. Jesus bent down to help humanity; so must we. Freely give to others in the way of our precious Lord Jesus. Jesus' example is our supreme pattern for godliness.

January 14

*And I will walk among you, and will be your God, and
ye shall be my people.*

Leviticus 26:12

Each life that touches ours for good is a
reflection of God's love for us. God never
stops telling us, "I love you." God invites us to run
into his protective embrace. Truly—God is our
benevolent provider!

January 15

And when Abram was ninety years old and nine, the LORD appeared to Abram, and said unto him, I am the Almighty God; walk before me, and be thou perfect. And I will make my covenant between me and thee, and will multiply thee exceedingly.

Genesis 17:1–2

Lord, focusing on your Word is a great blessing. The more I keep it before me, the more faithfully I walk in your ways. Help me to make the most of every opportunity I have to read, think about, and discuss the things you share with us through the Scriptures.

January 16

Blessed is the man that walketh not in the counsel of the ungodly, nor standeth in the way of sinners, nor sitteth in the seat of the scornful. But his delight is in the law of the LORD; and in his law doth he meditate day and night.

Psalm 1:1–2

God's highest priority is that we get to know him and live a life that reflects his love and justice. All who love are born of God. Love God first, follow his word, and all of your other relationships will fall into place.

January 17

The wicked walk on every side, when the vilest men are exalted.

Psalm 12:8

Lord, please keep me from saying one thing and doing another—like saying we are to love others, even those who are different, but turning away from or ridiculing them when I come face to face. Promises, empty promises, politics to pulpit to people around the table. Our values can be inverted and I'm numbed by how easily we don't mean what we say. God, help me to be consistent. Keep me authentic.

January 18

And if ye walk contrary unto me, and will not hearken unto me; I will bring seven times more plagues upon you according to your sins.

Leviticus 26:21

Lord, in my darkest moments, it is easy to despair and fear that you have given up on me. It would be understandable for you to be angry and disappointed and leave me to my ruin, sevenfold. But how comforting it is to know that the minute I regret what I have done and turn to you, you are right where you have been all along—by my side, ready to embrace and carry me until I am strong enough to take a step on my own. Thank you for your faithfulness, Lord—especially when I least deserve it.

January 19

Judge me, O LORD; for I have walked in mine integrity: I have trusted also in the LORD; therefore I shall not slide. Examine me, O LORD, and prove me; try my reins and my heart. For thy lovingkindness is before mine eyes: and I have walked in thy truth.

Psalm 26:1–3

Lord, how grateful I am that you are willing to go before me to prepare the way. Even when I sense that a new opportunity is from you and has your blessing, I've learned I still need to stop and ask you to lead before I take the first step. Otherwise I will stumble along in the dark tripping over stones of my own creation! Everything goes more smoothly when you are involved, Lord.

January 20

Then I saw that wisdom excelleth folly, as far as light excelleth darkness. The wise man's eyes are in his head; but the fool walketh in darkness.

Ecclesiastes 2:13–14

*L*ord, so often we find ourselves asking you to save us from bad situations only to discover you quietly revealing to us that we are our own worst enemies! Teach us to break destructive habits and to stop polluting our minds with negative thoughts, Lord. Save us from our enemies, even when it means you have to step in and save us from ourselves!

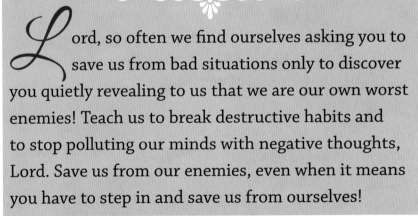

January 21

The just man walketh in his integrity: his children are blessed after him.

Proverbs 20:7

Whenever I worry that I don't know what I'm doing as a parent, I remind myself that God trusted me enough to make me a mother. His belief in me renews my belief in myself. My children make me strive to be the woman I've always wanted to be: strong, kind, patient, fun. With God's help, I can achieve this vision.

January 22

Teach me thy way, O LORD; I will walk in thy truth: unite my heart to fear thy name. I will praise thee, O Lord my God, with all my heart: and I will glorify thy name for evermore.

Psalm 86:11–12

I rest in God's peace, placing my faith entirely in his will for me. I relax in God's love, knowing he leads me towards my highest good. I give thanks for God's presence, understanding that it is the foundation of my spiritual wholeness within. I offer God all that I have for the eternal miracles he promises in return.

January 23

O LORD God of Israel, there is no God like thee in the heaven, nor in the earth; which keepest covenant, and shewest mercy unto thy servants, that walk before thee with all their hearts.

2 Chronicles 6:14

How good it is to know that God is on my side! Though my friends and my family may have my back, they can't always stop what they are doing to help me. But God can, and God does. Knowing he has faith in me allows me to have more faith in myself, to meet with any challenge and overcome any obstacle. How blessed I am to glow in the light of God's faith in me!

January 24

*Obey my voice, and I will be your God, and ye shall be my people:
and walk ye in all the ways that I have commanded you,
that it may be well unto you.*

Jeremiah 7:23

When you pray, don't forget to thank God for what you ask for. Better yet, thank God in advance for blessings yet to come, for this is a powerful way to show your faith. Instead of waiting until your prayer is answered, give thanks for God in all things and let your faith in him be strong and secure.

January 25

Through faith we understand that the worlds were framed by the word of God.

Hebrews 11:3

*L*ord, how we love to contemplate your sojourn on earth. How you came that we might see heaven in your eyes even as the earth was beneath your feet. How you were present in the lives of those who walked with you and attentive to the unspoken needs of every heart. How we love to tell of your sacrifice on the cross so that all of us might one day share eternal life with you. It's the story that never grows old, the only story that has the power to save, the power to transform hearts.

January 26

Rejoice, O young man, in thy youth; and let thy heart cheer thee in the days of thy youth, and walk in the ways of thine heart, and in the sight of thine eyes: but know thou, that for all these things God will bring thee into judgment. Therefore remove sorrow from thy heart, and put away evil from thy flesh: for childhood and youth are vanity.

Ecclesiastes 11:9–10

Beware of smugness and pride—do not let those vain feelings guide your actions. Instead, try to keep your thoughts and actions genuine, rather than using them to gain attention from others. If you lack control, ask God to show you how to become stronger. He will guide you with his strong, gentle hand.

January 27

I will pay my vows unto the LORD now in the presence of all his people.

Psalm 116:18

In all you do, have faith. In all you say and think and feel, have faith. Living in faith works on all levels, from the spiritual to the physical to the mental. Have faith in goodness, in light, and in love. Let it permeate every cell of your being. Then go out in the world and spread that goodness, that light, and that love. Be faith in human form.

January 28

That they may fear thee, to walk in thy ways, so long as they live in the land which thou gavest unto our fathers.

2 Chronicles 6:31

God doesn't always give us the blessings we think we must have. Instead, he asks us to simply have faith in his will for us, and believe that we will be given something better, something greater. Our focus may be limited, and our vision blocked, but God sees all and knows what miracles lay outside of our understanding. Trust God and have faith in his plan, even if it unfolds in a way you weren't expecting it to.

January 29

Now no chastening for the present seemeth to be joyous, but griev-ous: nevertheless afterward it yieldeth the peaceable fruit of righteousness unto them which are exercised thereby.

Hebrews 12:11

Every day I blow it. Every day I need your grace, Lord. I am thankful that it isn't necessary to live a perfect life to have access to your grace. If that were the case, I'd be in big trouble. But instead of turning your back on me when I veer from your paths, you are always ready to welcome me with open arms. You simply call me to trust in your saving, relationship-restoring grace. That's where I'm standing right now—in that amazing grace of yours, asking you to forgive and restore me once again so I can resume good fellowship with you.

January 30

Whoso walketh uprightly shall be saved: but he that is perverse in his ways shall fall at once.

Proverbs 28:18

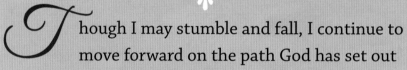

Though I may stumble and fall, I continue to move forward on the path God has set out for me. I walk in faith through the darkest valleys and over the biggest obstacles, staying focused on where he leads me. Though I may grow tired and weary, I continue on in faith that God will carry me in his arms when I cannot continue to walk on my own.

January 31

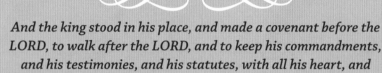

And the king stood in his place, and made a covenant before the LORD, to walk after the LORD, and to keep his commandments, and his testimonies, and his statutes, with all his heart, and with all his soul, to perform the words of the covenant which are written in this book.

2 Chronicles 34:31

When in doubt, find your faith. When in fear, find your faith. When in confusion, find your faith. Having a strong and unyielding faith in God can help you overcome anything life throws your way. It may require looking deep within, but sometimes you have to work to find it. Think of faith like a buried treasure that just requires a little digging to reach, but is so worth the effort.

February

February 1

Take ye heed every one of his neighbour, and trust ye not in any brother: for every brother will utterly supplant, and every neighbour will walk with slanders.

Jeremiah 9:4

People will let you down and disappoint you. That is part of being human. If we put our faith in other people, often we will be left frustrated and sad. But God does not let us down or disappoint us. During the times people are just not able to give us what we need, we can turn to God in faith and find clarity and strength again.

February 2

But as for me, I will walk in mine integrity: redeem me, and be merciful unto me. My foot standeth in an even place: in the congregations will I bless the LORD.

Psalm 26:11–12

Tear down your defenses and place your trust in people who love you. Keep your loved ones close and the Lord even closer. Sometimes the truth that we are not alone is a rope that keeps us from slipping, much as the rope climber clings to on the side of the mountain.

February 3

Follow peace with all men, and holiness, without which no man shall see the Lord.

Hebrews 12:14

Happiness comes to those who can let go of what they cannot control. Living from a place of faith eases the pressure of always knowing how to fix things and make them go our way. God alone has complete control. Faith in God brings peace to the spirit and the joy that comes from being able to go with the flow of life, knowing we are always cared for and guided.

February 4

Discretion shall preserve thee, understanding shall keep thee: To deliver thee from the way of the evil man, from the man that speaketh froward things; Who leave the paths of uprightness, to walk in the ways of darkness.

Proverbs 2:11–13

The best thing I ever did was discover a well-spring within of faith and trust in God. No matter what challenges I face, no matter who hurts me or how bad I feel, I know that all I need to do is get quiet and listen for that small, still voice within. That voice is God telling me I am loved, listened to, and cared for.

February 5

Wilt not thou deliver my feet from falling, that I may walk before God in the light of the living?

Psalm 56:13

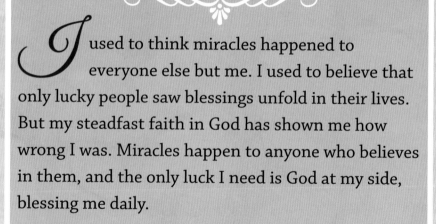

I used to think miracles happened to everyone else but me. I used to believe that only lucky people saw blessings unfold in their lives. But my steadfast faith in God has shown me how wrong I was. Miracles happen to anyone who believes in them, and the only luck I need is God at my side, blessing me daily.

February 6

Be not forgetful to entertain strangers: for thereby some have entertained angels unawares.

Hebrews 13:2

After you recover from a crisis, you are better able to help others. True faith is demonstrated when we look for ways to be kind to those in need. God strengthened you; now he can use you to strengthen others. In the presence of our compassion, Christ is made more meaningful to others. A life of compassion toward others is a life of reverence toward Christ.

February 7

For God shall bring every work into judgment, with every secret thing, whether it be good, or whether it be evil.

Ecclesiastes 12:14

We can never be completely honest on our own. It is human nature to lie. That's why when a witness who takes the stand in a court of law is asked, "Do you solemnly swear to tell the truth, the whole truth, and nothing but the truth," the phrase is added, "so help me God."

February 8

Blessed are they that keep his testimonies, and that seek him with the whole heart. They also do no iniquity: they walk in his ways.

Psalm 119:2–3

We think we know what is best for our lives, but sometimes God knows better. He can see the big picture while we only focus on the small details. Letting God's will play out in our lives requires a strong faith and the ability to just surrender—surrender our own stubborn will to the one who knows us best, and what is best for us.

February 9

For here have we no continuing city, but we seek one to come.
Hebrews 13:14

How tricky it can be to help our children fit into their world without becoming of the world. God can gently guide us as we guide their choices into what is safe and okay to "follow" and what is not. God never turns away from even the smallest concern, a lesson to teach daily.

February 10

So shalt thou find favour and good understanding in the sight of God and man. Trust in the LORD with all thine heart; and lean not unto thine own understanding.

Proverbs 3:3–4

How like a little boy I can be: Look, God, I'm all ready to do great things for you. I've got all the right credentials and intentions. Just watch me! Then fwomp! Down I go. But even while my wounds are stinging and my pride is still smarting, there is God comforting me, and his very presence brings me back to my senses, back to the humble dependence on him once again.

February 11

For man also knoweth not his time: as the fishes that are taken in an evil net, and as the birds that are caught in the snare; so are the sons of men snared in an evil time, when it falleth suddenly upon them.

Ecclesiastes 9:12

I cannot see the light, but I know it is just up ahead. I cannot find the way out, but I know that my path is leading me there. I cannot solve the problem, but I know the solution is on its way. I know these things because of my faith in God, who has never failed me, and never will.

February 12

Pleasant words are as an honeycomb, sweet to the soul,
and health to the bones.

Proverbs 16:24

Someone I care about is suffering, Lord, and I feel helpless. Assure me that a little "honey" means a lot and that I'm sharing your healing love in my notes and visits. If you need me to do more, send me. I am like dandelion fluff, small but mighty in possibility. Joyful is the one who, having been healed, also learns to go forth and heal others.

February 13

For there is not a just man upon earth, that doeth good, and sinneth not.

Ecclesiastes 7:20

I make mistakes and bad decisions. I screw up and hurt myself, as well as others. I say the wrong things at the wrong times. But God never stops having faith in me. No matter how much I mess up, God is there to help me get my life back on track. His faith in me is eternal and gives me the encouragement I need to make a fresh start out of each new day.

February 14

He that walketh uprightly walketh surely: but he that perverteth his ways shall be known.

Proverbs 10:9

If your own mind confuses you, and your own heart fails you, just ask God for help. If your spirit is weak, and your will is low, have faith that God will take control and let his will be done. If you doubt, fear or worry, turn it over to God and know that he is working towards your highest good, now and always.

February 15

Though I walk in the midst of trouble, thou wilt revive me: thou shalt stretch forth thine hand against the wrath of mine enemies, and thy right hand shall save me.

Psalm 138:7

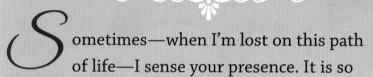

Sometimes—when I'm lost on this path of life—I sense your presence. It is so comforting to think of you searching tirelessly to find me again. Grant me your grace so I can stay on your paths more steadily. This way, you'll have more time to devote to searching out others!

February 16

Sorrow is better than laughter: for by the sadness of the countenance the heart is made better.

Ecclesiastes 7:3

Only when we are ready to relinquish the hurt is there an opportunity for forgiveness and healing to begin. Truly, forgiveness is a healing gift from above. If I'm honest with myself, I'll admit that the greatest joys in my life have sprung from the fertile grounds of suffering—but only after I have asked God to take charge of my garden of sorrow.

February 17

He that walketh with wise men shall be wise: but a companion of fools shall be destroyed.

Proverbs 13:20

I do sometimes prefer frivolity and flattery to growing in the light of some uncomfortable truth, Lord. You can see where I'm prone to skirting the issues I need to deal with, and you know when I'm indulging in foolishness when I could be having a meaningful interaction with someone who walks in the truth. I know it's okay to have fun, but it's good for me to look in the mirror regularly as well. Grant me the grace to soak in the wisdom that will change me for the better.

February 18

All the labour of man is for his mouth,
and yet the appetite is not filled.

Ecclesiastes 6:7

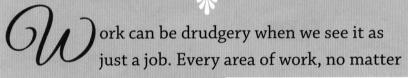

Work can be drudgery when we see it as just a job. Every area of work, no matter how insignificant it may seem, is an opportunity to faithfully serve God and others. We all want to do something effective in this world while we are here. The key is being faithful to what God lays on our heart.

February 19

As he came forth of his mother's womb, naked shall he return to go as he came, and shall take nothing of his labour, which he may carry away in his hand.

Ecclesiastes 5:15

When things go well, and we are prospering and happy, it's easy to forget that faith was how we got there — that faith is all we "carry away" from this life. We only recall this when all is lost. Life goes in cycles and we must learn to find faith in God and his mysterious ways when we are in a low cycle, because that is when we most need to hold steady and hang on. He will always lead us back into abundance again.

February 20

*If ye oppress not the stranger, the fatherless, and the widow, and
shed not innocent blood in this place, neither walk after other gods
to your hurt: Then will I cause you to dwell in this place, in the
land that I gave to your fathers, for ever and ever.*

Jeremiah 7:6–7

If you put your faith in the desires of people,
you will be disappointed. If you put your
faith in the motives of those you interact with, you
might be betrayed. But by putting your faith entirely
in God, and letting him direct the path you should
walk along, He will always be there to help steer you
clear of the people you are not meant to be with.
Remember, rejection is God's protection.

February 21

But they hearkened not, nor inclined their ear, but walked in the counsels and in the imagination of their evil heart, and went backward, and not forward.

Jeremiah 7:24

ruth is a narrow road, and it's easy to fall to one side or the other. For every beautiful kernel of truth, there are a thousand lies that can be made around it. Staying on the straight-and-narrow would be impossible if it weren't for the Spirit of God, who leads us to all truth. Delving into God's Word with the Holy Spirit to guide us is the best way to stay on track and keep walking in the truth.

February 22

O LORD, I know that the way of man is not in himself: it is not in man that walketh to direct his steps.

Jeremiah 10:23

An open door is an invitation. Just as the gates of Heaven are open to all who follows God's will, an open door invites me in to experience new joys and revelations. Thank you, God, for allowing me to see the open doors in my life and take advantage of new experiences. Let me walk through them with Jesus at my side.

February 23

Let, we beseech thee, our supplication be accepted before thee, and pray for us unto the LORD thy God, … That the LORD thy God may shew us the way wherein we may walk, and the thing that we may do.

Jeremiah 42:2–3

When we try to control every aspect of life, we are doing God's job. He alone is the micromanager. He alone knows what is best. Our job is to do what feels right in our hearts for that is his will speaking to us. There is no need to stress or worry, no need to force or push. Life flows when we put our faith where it belongs...in God.

February 24

They are not humbled even unto this day, neither have they feared, nor walked in my law, nor in my statutes, that I set before you and before your fathers.

Jeremiah 44:10

If I look back upon my life, I realize that the hardest times were when I had abandoned God. I felt lost and alone and so afraid. When I found my faith again and placed it back in God, my life began to turn itself around, as if by a miracle! But really that miracle was remembering God and acknowledging his love and presence. He never abandoned me, even when I lost faith in him.

February 25

For my people is foolish, they have not known me; they are sottish children, and they have none understanding: they are wise to do evil, but to do good they have no knowledge.

Jeremiah 4:22

I can complain about my life and wallow in unhappiness, or I can take action and have a bold faith that God has my back. I can stay stuck in a rut, miserable and whining, or I can move in the direction of God's loving guidance. I can give into weakness and lose all hope, or I can be strong in my faith and find the blessings amidst the lessons, the joys amidst the troubles.

February 26

Your iniquities have turned away these things, and your sins have withholden good things from you.

Jeremiah 5:25

We have good days and bad days, but if we keep our faith and our focus, we will have more good than bad. Faith during good times is easy, but the real test of our courage and resilience comes when the going gets rough. That's when we most need our faith to get going, and get us back to God.

February 27

*We looked for peace, but no good came; and for
a time of health, and behold trouble!*

Jeremiah 8:15

The true test of our love for God comes when things don't happen the way we want them to. When our faith falters, we are being called upon to find it again, even if we feel like giving up and giving in. Staying centered in faith helps to straighten what is crooked, and strengthen what is weak.

February 28

They are upright as the palm tree, but speak not: they must needs be borne, because they cannot go. Be not afraid of them; for they cannot do evil, neither also is it in them to do good.

Jeremiah 10:5

In our lives, other people, even circumstances, will hurt us. Many of us want to hang on and not let go of the past, because we think we can change it. But we can't. This is when we most need to let go and turn it over to God. Doing so gives us freedom of the mind, heart and spirit. God alone knows where our future will take us...if we first let go of the past.

March

March 1

Blessed is the man that trusteth in the LORD, and whose hope the LORD is.

Jeremiah 17:7

When nothing seems to be happening and your dreams appear to be forgotten, let go. When no one is there to support you and you feel like you can't count on anyone, let go. When life seems to have stopped in its tracks and you can't see the blocks, let go. Turn your faith to God and soon everything will be made right again. Sometimes, it takes an act of total surrender to open the closed doors in life.

March 2

Then I went down to the potter's house, and, behold, he wrought a work on the wheels. And the vessel that he made of clay was marred in the hand of the potter: so he made it again another vessel, as seemed good to the potter to make it. Then the word of the LORD came to me, saying, O house of Israel, cannot I do with you as this potter? saith the LORD. Behold, as the clay is in the potter's hand, so are ye in mine hand.

Jeremiah 18:3–6

We make our own plans, but it is God who leads the way and clears the obstacles from our path. When tempted to stubbornly think "I can do this myself" and "I don't need to pray or ask God about this," it's wise to remember that God has promised to guide—not "overrule"—us.

March 3

As for me, behold, I am in your hand: do with me as seemeth good and meet unto you.

Jeremiah 26:14

You have made things problematic again, Lord, and I need to see that all this upheaval can be a good thing. Help me, Lord. And thank you for showing me that a thoroughly comfortable existence can rob me of real life.

March 4

For I know the thoughts that I think toward you, saith the LORD, thoughts of peace, and not of evil, to give you an expected end. Then shall ye call upon me, and ye shall go and pray unto me, and I will hearken unto you. And ye shall seek me, and find me, when ye shall search for me with all your heart.

Jeremiah 29:11–13

Ask and you shall receive. Knock and the door will be open to you. The act of faith allows you to have the courage to ask and knock, and expect the door to be opened, revealing the blessings God has in store for you. So go ahead, don't be afraid. Have courage and ask. Have faith and knock. Then go through the door that appears before you.

March 5

Yea, I will rejoice over them to do them good, and I will plant them in this land assuredly with my whole heart and with my whole soul.

Jeremiah 32:41

The blessings of God are always available to us. But we have to believe we are worthy of them. God's love for us is unconditional. Can we accept that and allow in all of the miracles he has in store? Many of us have a hard time receiving. But just as God loves to give to us, he wants us to receive what he gives. It makes God happy when we enjoy the gifts of his presence.

March 6

And it shall be to me a name of joy, a praise and an honour before all the nations of the earth, which shall hear all the good that I do unto them: and they shall fear and tremble for all the goodness and for all the prosperity that I procure unto it.

Jeremiah 33:9

When we experience true joy, we will naturally express it. As God pours joy into our lives, we can bring it back to him. How wonderful that God wants us to go beyond the pursuit of happiness to experience joy. We can be joyful even when we're unhappy. We can maintain our joy when we remember how faithful and unchanging God is. Focusing on him brings renewed joy.

March 7

Whether it be good, or whether it be evil, we will obey the voice of the LORD our God, to whom we send thee; that it may be well with us, when we obey the voice of the LORD our God.

Jeremiah 42:6

God, shine your healing light down upon me today, for my path is filled with painful obstacles and my suffering fogs my vision. Clear the challenges from the road I must walk upon, or at least walk with me as I confront them. With you, I know I can endure anything. With you, I know I can make it through to the other side, where joy awaits.

March 8

For a bishop must be blameless, as the steward of God; not selfwilled, not soon angry, not given to wine, no striker, not given to filthy lucre; But a lover of hospitality, a lover of good men, sober, just, holy, temperate; Holding fast the faithful word as he hath been taught, that he may be able by sound doctrine both to exhort and to convince the gainsayers.

Titus 1:6–9

I may not always believe in myself, but I know God believes in me. His faith in me is what I lean on when I feel weak, afraid and alone. Each time I've been unsure of myself, God has pushed me to move forward, even in the smallest of ways. Each time I've been afraid to leave my comfort zone, God reminds me he is my comfort zone and to just have faith and take that first step.

March 9

For the grace of God that bringeth salvation hath appeared to all men, Teaching us that, denying ungodliness and worldly lusts, we should live soberly, righteously, and godly, in this present world; Looking for that blessed hope, and the glorious appearing of the great God and our Saviour Jesus Christ.

Titus 2:11–13

*L*oving someone asks that you assume they will love you in return. They don't always. Pursuing a goal asks that you believe you will achieve it. You may not. But true faith understands that you don't always get what you want in life, but that God provides you with what you need, and what will make you whole, happy and healthy. God knows best. Put your faith in him.

March 10

For we ourselves also were sometimes foolish, disobedient, deceived, serving divers lusts and pleasures, living in malice and envy, hateful, and hating one another. But after that the kindness and love of God our Saviour toward man appeared, That being justified by his grace, we should be made heirs according to the hope of eternal life.

Titus 3:3–4, 7

When everything seems hopeless and my heart is weary and tired, I reach deep within myself to find the stillness, where God's love awaits. In that peaceful place, I know that my faith in God will be rewarded, despite the pain and suffering I feel right now. In that loving warmth, I know my faith in God will be restored, and I will feel hope and happiness again.

March 11

But avoid foolish questions, and genealogies, and contentions, and strivings about the law; for they are unprofitable and vain.

Titus 3:9

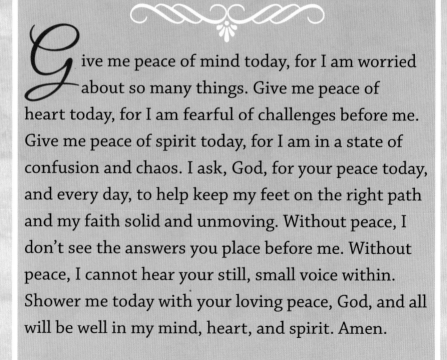

Give me peace of mind today, for I am worried about so many things. Give me peace of heart today, for I am fearful of challenges before me. Give me peace of spirit today, for I am in a state of confusion and chaos. I ask, God, for your peace today, and every day, to help keep my feet on the right path and my faith solid and unmoving. Without peace, I don't see the answers you place before me. Without peace, I cannot hear your still, small voice within. Shower me today with your loving peace, God, and all will be well in my mind, heart, and spirit. Amen.

March 12

And they sang together by course in praising and giving thanks unto the LORD; because he is good, for his mercy endureth for ever toward Israel. And all the people shouted with a great shout, when they praised the LORD, because the foundation of the house of the LORD was laid.

Ezra 3:11

Lord, how I pray that your love is evident in me today! I want to follow you closely and help draw others to you as well. I know that if those with whom I come in contact see love, joy, peace, patience, kindness, goodness, faithfulness, gentleness, and self-control in me, they may find you as well. Direct my steps as I follow you, Lord, and may the grace you've sprinkled on me be revealed for your glory. Amen.

March 13

For upon the first day of the first month began he to go up from Babylon ... according to the good hand of his God upon him. For Ezra had prepared his heart to seek the law of the LORD, and to do it, and to teach in Israel statutes and judgments.

Ezra 7:9–10

As much as I want to control my life, I know that I must let go of that need sometimes, especially during times of trouble. I can't fix things, but I know that God can, if I but put my faith and trust in him. Though the ways of God may be mysterious to me, I know they work, for they always have. Turning to God has never failed me before, and it won't fail me now.

March 14

And whatsoever shall seem good to thee, and to thy brethren,
to do with the rest of the silver and the gold, that do
after the will of your God.

Ezra 7:18

I love my friends and family and am blessed to have such wonderful people in my life. But often they are busy with their own challenges to help me face mine. That is when I turn to the one who never fails to be there when I call upon him. That is when I turn to God and put my trust and faith in him to give me strength and resourcefulness to overcome obstacles in my path. God is my rock and my foundation!

March 15

Arise; for this matter belongeth unto thee: we also will be with thee: be of good courage, and do it.

Ezra 10:3–4

Like a speed bump in a parking lot, a decision lies in our path, placed there by God to remind us hope is a choice. Choosing to live as people of hope is not to diminish or belittle pain and suffering or lie about evil's reality. Rather it is to cling to God's promise that he will make all things new.

March 16

Keep thy foot when thou goest to the house of God, and be more ready to hear, than to give the sacrifice of fools.

Ecclesiastes 5:1

Why am I so contrary at times? I wonder and worry. Perhaps it is tiredness, frustration, pressure, but too often I lose my cool and others do likewise until we have a mess and muddle. Life wears me down and I make misguided choices. I'm grateful and humbled that God can help repair them.

March 17

Be not rash with thy mouth, and let not thine heart be hasty to utter any thing before God: for God is in heaven, and thou upon earth: therefore let thy words be few.

Ecclesiastes 5:2

Watching the news can become an exercise in faith. There is so much bad in the world, so much evil. Yet we all too often forget that there is so much more good that we do not see. Building faith means focusing on the good things, and understanding that the bad things have their place in God's greater plan, even if we don't know how or why.

March 18

The sleep of a labouring man is sweet, whether he eat little or much: but the abundance of the rich will not suffer him to sleep.

Ecclesiastes 5:12

*L*ife is filled with times of failure and disappointment, when we don't quite get the outcomes we desired. It's easy during these times to doubt ourselves and our ability to be resilient and rise above the obstacles facing us. But God never loses faith in us. God always knows we have what it takes to find our wings and soar again, no matter how long we've been grounded.

March 19

Better is the sight of the eyes than the wandering of the desire: this is also vanity and vexation of spirit.

Ecclesiastes 6:9

The hardest times to have faith are the times we most need to trust God. His will may not be what we want for ourselves, but we have to believe that it is the best for us, even when it hurts and nothing seems to be going right. Having faith when it's dark means we will see the light of a new day, because God has never failed us before. He won't fail us now.

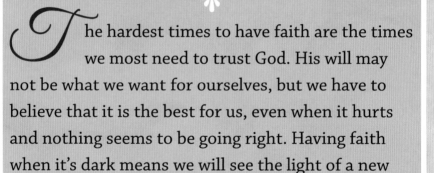

March 20

Consider the work of God: for who can make that straight, which he hath made crooked?

Ecclesiastes 7:13

When all seems lost, we must turn to God for support and love. When all seems hopeless, we must turn to God within and hold fast to our faith. When all seems bleak, we must listen for God's whispers of love and encouragement. God is always working for us, even when it appears we are alone.

March 21

A faithful man shall abound with blessings.

Proverbs 28:20

Permanence is hard to find in this world. Everything changes. People come and go. Jobs start and end. Desires and dreams shift. We get older and grow up and out of things. There is one thing, however, we can rest assured will never change or leave or disappear, and that is God's love for us, and faith in us.

March 22

He that giveth unto the poor shall not lack: but he that hideth his eyes shall have many a curse.

Proverbs 28:27

Faith is both a noun and a verb. It is something we have, and something we do. Having faith is our connection to God, but without doing something with that connection, we fail to see our blessings manifest. We don't feel happy and fulfilled. Putting our faith in action gives life meaning and purpose. It means what we do in the world really matters.

March 23

Correct thy son, and he shall give thee rest; yea, he shall give delight unto thy soul.

Proverbs 29:17

You are surrounded by love, and all it takes to see it and experience it is the faith that it is there. Open your eyes and your heart to the love all around, even amidst challenges and hard times, even with people who are difficult. Faith is what allows you to be aware of it, accepting of it, and grateful for it. Love is everywhere.

March 24

Every word of God is pure: he is a shield unto them that put their trust in him. Add thou not unto his words, lest he reprove thee, and thou be found a liar.

Proverbs 30:5–6

I put my faith in God, knowing that he alone knows best. I trust he will provide me with the next step I should take, and the next door I must enter, to bring about his will. Then I move forward. Though the path may not be visible to me at first, my faith means walking anyway. If I stay still, the path will never reveal itself.

March 25

Surely the churning of milk bringeth forth butter, and the wringing of the nose bringeth forth blood: so the forcing of wrath bringeth forth strife.

Proverbs 30:33

God stretches our heart's capacity when he tells us to love our enemies. Loving them proves that we belong to God, for he loves everyone, no matter what they have done. We do not naturally love like God does, but we can desire to grow in demonstrating his love to others. Our Christian fervor can be measured by our desire to grow in love, in spite of the struggles we will undoubtedly encounter.

March 26

For if we have been planted together in the likeness of his death, we shall be also in the likeness of his resurrection.

Romans 6:5

J am only as strong as my faith, so I must work each day to keep my faith strong. I do this by bringing God into my heart, and allowing him to work through me. I look not to outside things, but to God for my guidance, because outside things are often just illusions. God alone is the giver of my strength, and through my faith in him, I walk my path with boldness, hope and joyful expectation.

March 27

Therefore we are buried with him by baptism into death: that like as Christ was raised up from the dead by the glory of the Father, even so we also should walk in newness of life.

Romans 6:4

The heartbreak of rejection can cause such a deep grief we never think we will recover from. Letting go of someone we love, because they choose to be with another, is agonizing. But there is comfort in having faith that God's will is working for our benefit, and that rejection is his protection. God knows best and having faith in him will lead us to one day love again.

March 28

*For sin shall not have dominion over you: for ye are
not under the law, but under grace.*

Romans 6:14

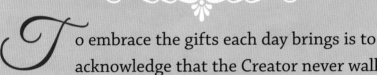

To embrace the gifts each day brings is to
acknowledge that the Creator never walks
away from his creation. Rather, his hand is always at
work making us better than we know we can be.

March 29

What then? shall we sin, because we are not under the law, but under grace? God forbid.

Romans 6:15

It's easy to have faith when things are going well and you can see how God is working miracles in your life. But true faith is forever, through the good times and the bad, through the times of plenty and the times of lack. Let your faith never waver, even when things look dark and bleak, because God is always working behind the scenes. The dawn always follows the night when your faith endures.

March 30

Being then made free from sin, ye became the servants of righteousness.

Romans 6:18

When I try to do something, I often fail. Trying is not enough, for I must believe with all my heart that I can succeed. Belief is a superpower given to us from a God who knows that by putting our utmost faith in him, we can achieve anything we set our minds and our hearts to.

March 31

But now being made free from sin, and become servants to God, ye have your fruit unto holiness, and the end everlasting life.

Romans 6:22

Having faith the size of a mustard seed is all we need to move the mountains of our lives. But do we truly believe this to be possible? Doubting takes us out of the power of faith. Fear destroys faith. Only when we stay centered in the truth that God is always working in our favor will we move those mountains. It all starts with faith.

April

April 1

For the wages of sin is death; but the gift of God is eternal life through Jesus Christ our Lord.

Romans 6:23

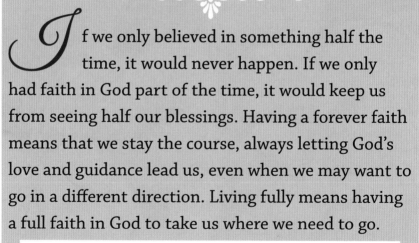

If we only believed in something half the time, it would never happen. If we only had faith in God part of the time, it would keep us from seeing half our blessings. Having a forever faith means that we stay the course, always letting God's love and guidance lead us, even when we may want to go in a different direction. Living fully means having a full faith in God to take us where we need to go.

April 2

There is therefore now no condemnation to them which are in Christ Jesus, who walk not after the flesh, but after the Spirit.

Romans 8:1

Genuine love for others begins with love for God. Our joy in God's love increases when we share it with others. Lifting others up in prayer is an exercise in faith. The blessing of faith in the Lord is salvation. Joy unites the hearts of all who rejoice in and are saved by Jesus.

April 3

For the law of the Spirit of life in Christ Jesus hath made me free from the law of sin and death.

Romans 8:2

It's often said that prayer changes things. This is true, but more importantly, prayer changes us. God is poised to save all who call on him. Renewal in the Lord has brought us unspeakable joy. The object of our gratitude should always be the Lord.

April 4

For they that are after the flesh do mind the things of the flesh; but they that are after the Spirit the things of the Spirit.

Romans 8:5

The passing of a dear one often leaves us wondering "Why, God, why?" If we knew that death is the beginning of a new mystery, a new adventure to unfold, we would feel joy for those who leave this earth and joy for those yet to leave. That simply isn't human nature. Help me understand that what may appear to be a "goodbye" is really only an "until we meet again." Amen.

April 5

For to be carnally minded is death; but to be spiritually minded is life and peace.

Romans 8:6

Perhaps we need to rethink our idea of what "peace" really is. God is always ready to give us true peace, if we are willing to ask him for it. Be at peace with God, and he will defeat the worldly beast within. God's peace is promised and proclaimed.

April 6

So then they that are in the flesh cannot please God.

Romans 8:8

Growing older doesn't necessitate letting go of faith. Even though our bodies are getting older and our thinking may not be as sharp as it once was, God is still the same. We can always depend on him. Our flesh is weak and impermanent, but our eternal life in God will always be unhindered.

April 7

But ye are not in the flesh, but in the Spirit, if so be that the Spirit of God dwell in you.

Romans 8:9

The people I know who walk in the ways of God are savory with the fruit of God's Spirit; they're the kind of people I can't be around enough. Their kind and gentle ways radiate peace. Their joy is contagious. Their faithfulness is inspiring. So many things about them make me want to be more like them—and more like Christ.

April 8

And if Christ be in you, the body is dead because of sin; but the Spirit is life because of righteousness.

Romans 8:10

Rarely do I consider myself particularly righteous, but then I remember that your Word says that I've been made righteous in Christ. It's not my righteousness that I'm counting on, but his. He is working his righteousness into my life day by day, but it's always his—not mine. That is reassuring and exciting! So even my prayers, as I walk in Christ's righteousness, can be powerful and effective...right here and now!

April 9

For if ye live after the flesh, ye shall die: but if ye through the Spirit do mortify the deeds of the body, ye shall live.

Romans 8:13

It is easy to have self-pity and resent the painful trials and heartaches that come into our lives. But God always works for our greater good. Pray that you will be God's instrument for bringing good to your world. Let the beams of God's goodness shine through you. Live through the Spirit.

April 10

For ye have not received the spirit of bondage again to fear; but ye have received the Spirit of adoption, whereby we cry, Abba, Father.

Romans 8:15

Imagine you are in a boat on the ocean. Suddenly the waters become choppy and you have a hard time keeping the boat afloat. As the waters grow rougher, you lose more and more control of the wheel that can turn the boat towards calmer waters. Letting our Holy Father take the wheel requires tremendous faith, but the results are tremendous peace. Let God steer.

April 11

The Spirit itself beareth witness with our spirit,
that we are the children of God.

Romans 8:16

Sometimes love seems so hard to find, and we are alone in a world full of couples. We feel flawed, and unlovable, as if there is no lid to our pot. But God wants us to know that we are surrounded by love, and no matter how long it takes, having faith in him will lead us to the people we are meant to have in our lives, no matter what form that may take.

April 12

For I reckon that the sufferings of this present time are not worthy to be compared with the glory which shall be revealed in us.

Romans 8:18

I know my strength, hope and courage come from God. I know that the peace that passes all understanding is available to me when I live in God's will. I know that I am loved and cared for by a God who never fails me. My faith is deep. My faith is solid. My faith is forever.

April 13

For we know that the whole creation groaneth and travaileth in pain together until now.

Romans 8:22

Too many times we set aside our faith for when life brings pain and suffering, because that is when we most need help. Jesus Christ brought an end to the "groans and travails" of humankind, but God wants us to have faith even when we are happy. Showing faith in good times is a form of gratitude, and a way to thank God for all the wonderful things we have been given.

April 14

And not only they, but ourselves also, which have the firstfruits of the Spirit, even we ourselves groan within ourselves, waiting for the adoption, to wit, the redemption of our body.

Romans 8:23

From the moment we are born, God is beside us, helping to guide us through life's ups and downs. From the day we become aware of his presence, we realize there is little to fear, if we give him control and follow his will. Living in this faith, we find that hard times become easier and challenges transform into lessons. Living in this faith, we are filled with gratitude and joy.

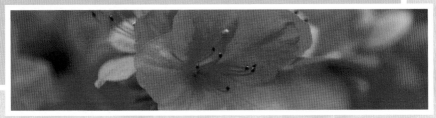

April 15

For we are saved by hope: but hope that is seen is not hope: for what a man seeth, why doth he yet hope for?

Romans 8:24

In order to truly be happy, we must believe that our faith will lead to blessings perfect for us. Giving thanks in advance shows God that we have the spirit of faith and a strong enough trust in him to be grateful even when we haven't been given anything yet. Believing in his goodness is receiving his goodness.

April 16

*But if we hope for that we see not, then do
we with patience wait for it.*

Romans 8:25

When love seems to have abandoned you, and you feel lost and alone, turn within and find the faith that has gotten you through all the challenges of the past. It is always there, waiting to be re-activated. Ask God to show you the way out, and know in faith that he will never let you down. Love, and life, will be filled with light again. Have faith!

April 17

Likewise the Spirit also helpeth our infirmities: for we know not what we should pray for as we ought: but the Spirit itself maketh intercession for us with groanings which cannot be uttered.

Romans 8:26

The Lord heals us in the time of our affliction. Pain can be a signal, a reminder to reach out to God for help. Let us always act on that signal. Give up struggling with the Lord and rest in his hands. Give the Lord your worries, and then let him keep them. The blessing of God's forgiveness is that he heals our wounds.

April 18

And we know that all things work together for good to them that love God, to them who are the called according to his purpose.

Romans 8:28

No matter where I am or what I am doing, I am never alone. God walks beside me, faithful and true. I know that I have his power to guide and direct my actions, and his love to shelter me from the storms of life. I know that I have everything I need in him to be happy, healthy and whole. I put my faith in his eternal love and care and I know I can do anything.

April 19

What shall we then say to these things? If God be for us, who can be against us?

Romans 8:31

There are times in life when having faith in myself has gotten me through. There are times when putting my faith in friends and family helped me move forward. But putting my faith in God alone has proven to be the one thing I can do to assure I am always loved, guided and protected.

April 20

Who shall lay any thing to the charge of
God's elect? It is God that justifieth.

Romans 8:33

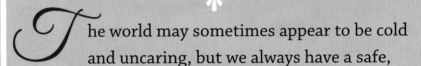

The world may sometimes appear to be cold and uncaring, but we always have a safe, warm place of peace within. That place is where God lives inside of us, loving us as a kind and supportive Father. When we have faith in God, nothing outside of us can truly do us harm, for we are always protected, always accepted.

April 21

Nay, in all these things we are more than conquerors through him that loved us.

Romans 8:37

No matter what challenges lay before you, count on God to help you overcome them. No matter your worries or concerns, count on God to guide you to the best solutions and bring you back into his peace. No matter how afraid you feel, turn it over to God. Have faith, for you never walk through this life alone!

April 22

For I am persuaded, that neither death, nor life, nor angels, nor principalities, nor powers, nor things present, nor things to come, Nor height, nor depth, nor any other creature, shall be able to separate us from the love of God, which is in Christ Jesus our Lord.

Romans 8:38–39

Storms may be brewing all around you, tossing you up and down upon the wild ocean waves. Having faith in God during the toughest of storms keeps you focused on the beacon of light that guides you back to the safety of the solid shore. Hold fast to God during the darkest of times. Your faith will bring you home again.

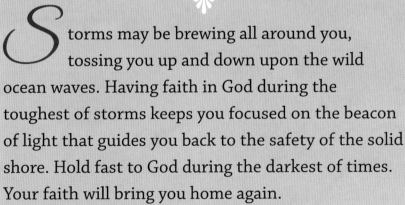

April 23

The LORD will not suffer the soul of the righteous to famish: but he casteth away the substance of the wicked.

Proverbs 10:3

Like a warm and cuddly blanket that makes a child feel secure, and a favorite food that soothes the worried soul, God is there for me. Like a song that lifts my spirits when nothing else can, and the laughter of a child that makes me laugh in return, God is my rock. I always put my faith in the one who never fails me. I put my faith in God.

April 24

*The blessing of the LORD, it maketh rich,
and he addeth no sorrow with it.*

Proverbs 10:22

Life is full of trade-offs, Lord, and I need to
make one. I want to venture off the fast track
where I'm losing more than I'm gaining. Guide my
search for a job where I can have both a life and a
living. Restore my balance, not the checkbook kind,
for it will change when I do. Your balance is not
found running in a circle, but along a beckoning path
where enough is more than sufficient; where money
comes second to family, community, and self; where
success takes on new meaning; and where, in the
giving up, I gain wealth beyond belief.

April 25

The way of the LORD is strength to the upright: but destruction shall be to the workers of iniquity.

Proverbs 10:29

God's promise to us is this: We will see it when we believe it. For God's blessings to appear in our lives, we must first have the steadfast faith that they have already been given to us. If we believe with every fiber of our being, God rewards our faith by giving us blessings, even ones we may not expect!

April 26

The righteous is delivered out of trouble,
and the wicked cometh in his stead.

Proverbs 11:8

Just because God's way of helping us is different than we hoped or expected, it doesn't mean he is indifferent to our cries for help. We must believe that he knows what is truly best for us and is actively doing what is best for us. Gently lead those who are hurting toward God's strength and compassion. Be like Christ—strong and gentle!

April 27

A false balance is abomination to the LORD:
but a just weight is his delight.

Proverbs 11:1

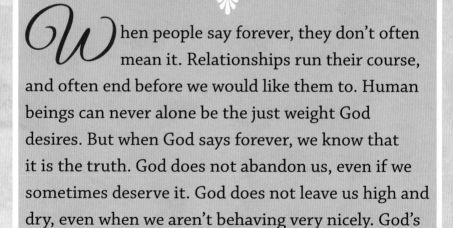

When people say forever, they don't often mean it. Relationships run their course, and often end before we would like them to. Human beings can never alone be the just weight God desires. But when God says forever, we know that it is the truth. God does not abandon us, even if we sometimes deserve it. God does not leave us high and dry, even when we aren't behaving very nicely. God's love is forever, and our faith in him never fails us.

April 28

The fruit of the righteous is a tree of life;
and he that winneth souls is wise.

Proverbs 11:30

When a task requiring faith confronts us, voices around us may say, "It can't be done." The voice may even come from within us, and we may want to quit before we start. But if we hold on to faith, we can succeed, no matter what the critics say.

April 29

Whoso loveth instruction loveth knowledge:
but he that hateth reproof is brutish.

Proverbs 12:1

very day is a journey through time and space. Thank you, Lord, for the journeys that make up my life and take me to amazing places. I am grateful for the things I've learned on my life's journey. Allow me to appreciate the journey more than the destination and keep an open mind for the unexpected gifts on the road. I may not always end up where I thought I would, but I am grateful for the paths I travel!

April 30

*Open thy mouth, judge righteously, and
plead the cause of the poor and needy.*

Proverbs 31:9

J esus healed the downcast, hurting, and rejected; so must we! God calls us to do special work. He supplies us with spiritual gifts to minister to spiritual needs.

May

May 1

Enter not into the path of the wicked, and go not in the way of evil men. Avoid it, pass not by it, turn from it, and pass away.

Proverbs 4:14–15

Not everything in life will go the way I want it. Not every person will have my highest good in mind. I can't get every need fulfilled unless I turn to God and have faith in him alone. That is when my life has a nice flow to it. It feels more meaningful and purposeful. That is when I know I am on the right track. I let God drive the car, and sit back and enjoy the ride!

May 2

My son, attend to my words; incline thine ear unto my sayings. Let them not depart from thine eyes; keep them in the midst of thine heart.

Proverbs 4:20

In this time of great change, help me, God of tomorrow, tomorrow, and tomorrow, to trust your guiding presence. Inspire me to follow with just enough light for the next step. Keep your Word front and center in my vision for my life. That's all I really need.

May 3

Put away from thee a froward mouth, and perverse lips put far from thee. Let thine eyes look right on, and let thine eyelids look straight before thee.

Proverbs 4:24–25

*L*ord, lead us past the temptation to sleep on the job, literally and figuratively. Grant us the good sense to know when to lock up and go home. There's nothing like a good night's sleep in our own beds, surrounded by snoring family, to get us ready for tomorrow, refreshed and eager for your call to excellence.

May 4

Ponder the path of thy feet, and let all thy ways be established. Turn not to the right hand nor to the left: remove thy foot from evil.

Proverbs 4:26–27

I may lose faith and hope when a relationship goes wrong or comes to an end. But I never lose faith and hope in the love of God. His love is unceasing and never-ending, and I can rely on it all the days of my life. His love is unconditional, and no matter what I do, I have his forgiveness. I put my faith first in God's love before others.

May 5

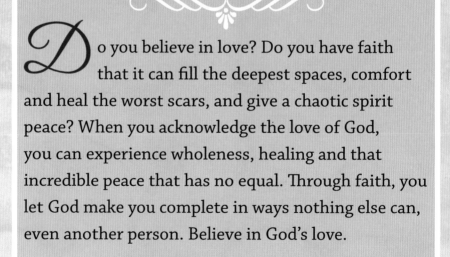

My son, keep thy father's commandment, and forsake not the law of thy mother: Bind them continually upon thine heart, and tie them about thy neck. When thou goest, it shall lead thee; when thou sleepest, it shall keep thee; and when thou awakest, it shall talk with thee. For the commandment is a lamp; and the law is light

Proverbs 6:20–23

Do you believe in love? Do you have faith that it can fill the deepest spaces, comfort and heal the worst scars, and give a chaotic spirit peace? When you acknowledge the love of God, you can experience wholeness, healing and that incredible peace that has no equal. Through faith, you let God make you complete in ways nothing else can, even another person. Believe in God's love.

May 6

Can a man take fire in his bosom, and his clothes not be burned?

Proverbs 6:27

Lead me not into temptation, O God, the daily ones, like keeping money I find, or exaggerating a headache into an excuse, or leaving racist remarks unchallenged. Small temptations, are they too trifling to worry about? It is tempting to think so, for I could easily go from occasional to habitual, from small to big. Keep me consistent in what I say and do, but stay nearby — I feel a little weak-kneed.

May 7

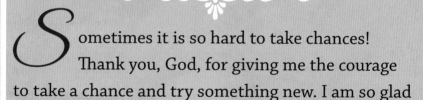

Hear instruction, and be wise, and refuse it not. Blessed is the man that heareth me, watching daily at my gates, waiting at the posts of my doors. For whoso findeth me findeth life, and shall obtain favour of the LORD.

Proverbs 8:33–35

Sometimes it is so hard to take chances! Thank you, God, for giving me the courage to take a chance and try something new. I am so glad to be able to step out of my comfort zone and find the courage to change. What a gift to know that taking a chance could change my life! Thank you for the excitement of being brave.

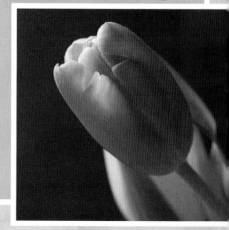

May 8

Thou compassest my path and my lying down, and art acquainted with all my ways. For there is not a word in my tongue, but, lo, O LORD, thou knowest it altogether.

Psalm 139:3–4

How often do we make plans, only to have them fall apart? When my day doesn't turn out the way I planned, it's easy to become angry. Instead, I look for ways to make the day special in a different way and thank God for showing me a new path. Lord, teach me to have a flexible heart and be willing to spend my time as you see fit, not as I do, and to open my eyes to the beauty of the unexpected.

May 9

When my spirit was overwhelmed within me, then thou knewest my path. In the way wherein I walked have they privily laid a snare for me. I looked on my right hand, and beheld, but there was no man that would know me: refuge failed me; no man cared for my soul. I cried unto thee, O LORD: I said, Thou art my refuge and my portion in the land of the living.

Psalm 142:3–5

When my faith is running low, I know I need to stop at a faith station and fill up my tank. My spirit is like a car that needs quality gasoline to run efficiently and get me where I need to go. So I turn to God, and let my faith be the fuel that moves me forward and guides me along the path of life.

May 10

Attend unto my cry; for I am brought very low: deliver me from my persecutors; for they are stronger than I.

Psalm 142:6

How wonderful it is to know that no matter what life throws my way, I can handle it! God never gives me more than I can handle, and he is always there to help me through the times I feel lost and alone. I have unceasing faith as I go about my day that all will be provided for, and that I will be guided and cared for in any situation.

May 11

Bring my soul out of prison, that I may praise thy name: the righteous shall compass me about; for thou shalt deal bountifully with me.

Psalm 142:7

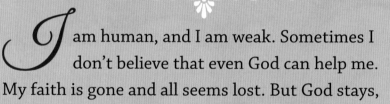

I am human, and I am weak. Sometimes I don't believe that even God can help me. My faith is gone and all seems lost. But God stays, reminding me that faith is a seed within that needs only a tiny bit of nurturing to grow again. God remains, showing me that even when I am faithless in him, he is faithful to me.

May 12

Preserve me, O God: for in thee do I put my trust.

Psalm 16:1

Your life is like a blank canvas, and you and God are the artists. When you work with God, putting your faith and trust in him to pick the right colors and the correct brushes, the result can be a beautiful masterpiece and the perfect creation of a life well-lived.

May 13

I will bless the LORD, who hath given me counsel.

Psalm 16:7

Many of us pray in the morning, and at night before we go to sleep. But we can be in prayer all throughout the day, living our lives aligned with God's love and will. All we need to do is walk in faith, casting aside fear, doubt and insecurity, for God always walks beside us.

May 14

I have set the LORD always before me: because he is at my right hand, I shall not be moved.

Psalm 16:8

There will be days when all you can do is cry and hang on tightly to your pillow. There will be nights that seem as though they will never end. These are the times when you most need to reach out to God. Search deep within and let your faith come to your rescue, for God is always with you. Let your faith strengthen, for you will see the light of a new day again.

May 15

Thou wilt shew me the path of life: in thy presence is fulness of joy
Psalm 16:11

To have hope is to put our life into the hands of a loving God that is always looking out for us, always making clear our path. When we are feeling down and about to give up, hope is like the sign on the road that tells us "rest stop ahead," and suddenly we feel renewed and refreshed, able to walk on just a bit longer and just a bit farther than we thought we could alone.

May 16

Concerning the works of men, by the word of thy lips I have kept me from the paths of the destroyer. Hold up my goings in thy paths, that my footsteps slip not.

Psalm 17:4–5

There will be days when your faith is as strong as a rock, and days when it is fluid like water. Some days it will be invisible like the air you breathe. But don't be afraid or depressed, because just as the air is ever-present, so is your faith. Just dig a little deeper, reach a little higher, walk a little farther and it is there, waiting for you.

May 17

As for me, I will behold thy face in righteousness: I shall be satisfied, when I awake, with thy likeness.

Psalm 17:15

Joy excludes none, for God's love invites us all. In the eyes of those we love we see the reflection of God looking back at us, smiling. This is what it means to feel and to know joy.

May 18

*I have called upon thee, for thou wilt hear me, O God:
incline thine ear unto me, and hear my speech.*

Psalm 17:6

When I pray to God, I don't always want something. Often, I just want to connect to that presence, that flow of love and life that permeates my spirit. When I meditate, I listen for God speaking to me within, and I take what he tells me so I may go out into the world, faith in hand, and act upon it. God is the flow of love through my mind, heart and spirit.

May 19

He restoreth my soul: he leadeth me in the paths of righteousness for his name's sake.

Psalm 23:3

There are times when all you can do is hold onto yourself and cry it out. Life can deal some hard blows, and it will hurt. But know that God is still there, watching over you. It may be hard to understand why these things happen, but God's plan is always in your favor. Rest in that and stay in your faith. The sun will shine again.

May 20

Shew me thy ways, O LORD; teach me thy paths.

Psalm 25:4

To walk in faith means to always believe that things are working for my highest good. To walk in faith means to rely on God and not try to force the outcome of things I cannot control. To walk in faith means to let go and relax, with no resistance towards what comes my way. To walk in faith means to lean on God for strength, hope and encouragement.

May 21

Lead me in thy truth, and teach me: for thou art the God of my salvation; on thee do I wait all the day.

Psalm 25:5

What does it mean to have faith? It means moving through the challenges of daily life with boldness because we know that someone has our back. It means approaching life's obstacles with courage and conviction because we know someone is looking out for us. It means walking with our heads held high because we know someone walks with us. That someone is God.

May 22

Remember, O LORD, thy tender mercies and thy loving kindnesses; for they have been ever of old.

Psalm 25:6

Heavenly Father, your son, Jesus, could have called down heaven to destroy his enemies when he was on earth, but he didn't. Revenge wasn't his mission. Love was. Help me to submit, as he did, to a path of gentleness in the strength of your love. Amen.

May 23

Remember not the sins of my youth, nor my transgressions: according to thy mercy remember thou me for thy goodness' sake, O LORD.

Psalm 25:7

When straying from God, it's reassuring to know there is no distance so great that can't be bridged. Tell God and others how you feel because, if you voice your pain, it can be whisked away in the wind. What a marvelous firsthand lesson to pass on.

May 24

Good and upright is the LORD: therefore will he teach sinners in the way

Psalm 25:8

Each day is a new beginning and a chance to do things differently. Each sunrise is an opportunity to heal the past and face the future with excitement and confidence. With faith in God, we can go forward and be open to anything that happens, knowing that it will either be a blessing to us, or a lesson for us.

May 25

For thy name's sake, O LORD, pardon mine iniquity; for it is great.

Psalm 25:11

The death of a loved one is a time of deep suffering and sometimes we lose our way entirely. We rage and lash out against God, because we don't understand why we had to lose someone we love. But God can take our anger and pain, and by having faith in him and his ways, we begin to find some healing and hope. We will never forget the ones we lose, but we will live, and even be happy, again.

May 26

Mine eyes are ever toward the LORD; for he shall pluck my feet out of the net.

Psalm 25:15

To have faith is to have the promise of God's love to see you through any situation in life. Faith accompanies us, helping us to see the next step along the unseen path that is his will. When we step out of faith, we step away from the peace and comfort of God. Walking in faith is walking with God.

May 27

Turn thee unto me, and have mercy upon me;
for I am desolate and afflicted.

Psalm 25:16

The Lord will weep with you during your darkest hour. Open the curtains and let God's light shine through the window to your soul. Give up your burdens to the Lord, and he will carry you in his heart. Our delight in God's love cannot compare with his joy in loving us. God's blessing of joy replaces our sorrow.

May 28

The troubles of my heart are enlarged:
O bring thou me out of my distresses.

Psalm 25:17

Through the darkest days, God walks beside me and will never leave me. His presence comforts me and gives me the courage to keep going no matter what the circumstances are. Through the darkest days, God walks beside us.

May 29

Look upon mine affliction and my pain; and forgive all my sins.

Psalm 25:18

The comfort of the Lord is truly trustworthy. God promises companionship through the valleys that inevitably brush the family, even if only on primetime, distant news or through neighborhood betrayals, or—God forbid— closer to home.

May 30

O keep my soul, and deliver me: let me not be ashamed; for I put my trust in thee.

Psalm 25:20

Gratitude is a wonderful way to show God how much we appreciate the blessings he bestows upon us. We can always find things to be grateful for, and even thank God in advance for blessings to come. That is the power of a living faith—showing we are thankful for things we cannot see yet. It shows we trust God to always provide more, but only when we are happy with what we already have.

May 31

Let integrity and uprightness preserve me; for I wait on thee.

Psalm 25:21

When your dreams seem so far away, and you feel ready to give up, that is when you finally realize that God alone can steer you in the direction of what you desire. Resisting and doubting blocks the flow of God's love, so let those gates of faith swing open wide, and trust God to do what is necessary to bring you closer to achieving your goals and living your dreams.

June

June 1

The LORD is my light and my salvation; whom shall I fear?
Psalm 27:1

When disaster strikes our lives, God is our rock, and nothing can separate us from him. Indeed, nothing can separate us from his love. To comfort others as Christ has comforted you is to be his hands reaching down from heaven. Christians are people of action because God is at work in them.

June 2

The LORD is the strength of my life; of whom shall I be afraid?

Psalm 27:1

No matter the difficult people who cross our paths, there is goodness in this world. It is there because we are surrounded by the goodness of God and the goodness he helps us cultivate in ourselves.

June 3

Unto thee will I cry, O LORD my rock; be not silent to me: lest, if thou be silent to me, I become like them that go down into the pit.

Psalm 28:1

Life has a rhythm, and if we get quiet enough, our spirit can hear it and move along with it. That rhythm is God's loving guidance, and we can step out in faith to the beat of that rhythm any time we want. It doesn't mean life will always be easy, but it does mean life won't ever give us anything we cannot handle with God right there beside us.

June 4

Hear the voice of my supplications, when I cry unto thee,
when I lift up my hands toward thy holy oracle.

Psalm 28:2

Bless the unknown angels who clear the cluttered paths of the lost, who wipe the tears of the grieving, and who hold the hands that tremble in fear. Their names may be known only to you, but their acts of mercy give me the assurance that your love touches everyone, everywhere.

June 5

Draw me not away with the wicked, and with the workers of iniquity, which speak peace to their neighbors, but mischief is in their hearts.

Psalm 28:3

Help me balance compassion with accountability as I work through this problem, Lord. This prayer has no end, for I need to work through the crisis and find a way out. Help me, and soon, for there are real wounds in your world to heal, not just my own hurt feelings.

June 6

*Blessed be the LORD, because he hath heard
the voice of my supplications.*

Psalm 28:6

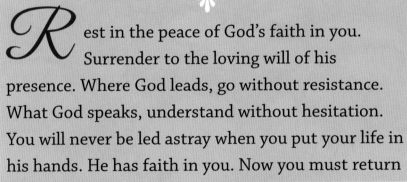

Rest in the peace of God's faith in you. Surrender to the loving will of his presence. Where God leads, go without resistance. What God speaks, understand without hesitation. You will never be led astray when you put your life in his hands. He has faith in you. Now you must return that faith and let him move through you in all your words, actions and thoughts. Be at peace.

June 7

The LORD is my strength and my shield; my heart trusted in him, and I am helped: therefore my heart greatly rejoiceth; and with my song will I praise him.

Psalm 28:7

No house can stand without a firm foundation. Upon the foundation all else is built. My faith is like that. If it is not firm and strong, nothing else good can come into my life. I must always turn to God as the firmament upon which my life is built, and put my faith in him. Without it, my walls and windows and doors will not function properly. God is my faith and my foundation.

June 8

*The LORD is their strength, and he is the
saving strength of his anointed.*

Psalm 28:8

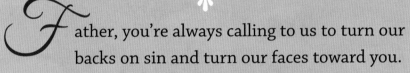

Father, you're always calling to us to turn our backs on sin and turn our faces toward you. You even promise to give us your own Spirit to lead and guide us and strengthen us to walk in your ways. I praise you today for your tireless love and concern for all people and for reaching out to us with your message of salvation.

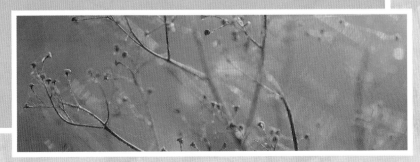

June 9

Reprove not a scorner, lest he hate thee:
rebuke a wise man, and he will love thee.

Proverbs 9:8

When a fish tries to swim against the current, it feels the power of resistance keep it from getting to where it needs to go. When I resist God's will and rely on myself, I swim against the stream and life is harder. I experience more fear, doubt and misery. Faith allows me to adjust my direction and go with the flow of life, and God's guidance. Faith lets me relax, knowing I am going where I need to be.

June 10

Give instruction to a wise man, and he will be yet wiser:
teach a just man, and he will increase in learning.

Proverbs 9:9

Listening with full attention is the first step toward a true relationship with God. Yet too often my love for God takes a backseat to my work and play. I don't want that to happen today. Father in heaven, please grant me the grace to love you fully.

June 11

The fear of the LORD is the beginning of wisdom: and the knowledge of the holy is understanding.

Proverbs 9:10

Walk along with God, hand in hand, for he alone knows the way. Put your faith in God, heart to heart, for he alone is eternal and unceasing love. Listen for his guidance and direction, for he sees the bigger picture of your life. Stay in his presence, for it is the solid foundation upon which all of your dreams are built.

June 12

For by me thy days shall be multiplied, and the years of thy life shall be increased.

Proverbs 9:11

Lord, today I ask your special blessing on the elderly among us. No matter how old we are, we notice our bodies aging. How difficult it must be to be near the end of life and struggling to hold on to mobility, vision, hearing, and wellness of being. Give us compassion for those older than we are, Lord, and thank you for your promise that you will be with us to the very end of our days.

June 13

If thou be wise, thou shalt be wise for thyself: but if thou scornest, thou alone shalt bear it.

Proverbs 9:12

*L*ord, it is tempting and easy to cast a scornful eye on those around us and note every fault. When my pride tempts me to do so, prompt me to turn the magnifying glass on myself instead. If I keep in mind how much I need your forgiveness every day, my love for you will never grow cold. I know you are willing to forgive each and every fault if I only ask you.

June 14

Then Peter said, Silver and gold have I none; but such as I have give I thee: In the name of Jesus Christ of Nazareth rise up and walk.

Acts 3:6

My trust is in you, God of miracles and surprises, for I feel your presence in so many ways. You call me to courage, but incrementally, as a believer emboldened to walk one step at a time.

June 15

Therefore thou art inexcusable, O man, whosoever thou art that judgest: for wherein thou judgest another, thou condemnest thyself; for thou that judgest doest the same things.

Romans 2:1

God of justice, we confess that we are too quick at times to judge those around us, basing our opinions not upon what is written in their hearts but what is easily seen by our lazy eyes. Keep us faithful to challenge one another any time we find ourselves speaking in generalities about any group of people or repeating jokes and slurs that offend and degrade.

June 16

To them who by patient continuance in well doing seek
for glory and honour and immortality, eternal life.

Romans 2:7

MY AIM IS...

to please him through communing in prayer

to show his love and for others care

to read his Word as my guide for life

to cease my grumbling that causes strife

to be open to God's leading and his will

to take time to meditate, be quiet, and still

to continually grow in my Christlike walk

to be more like Jesus in my life and my talk.

June 17

For when we were yet without strength, in due time Christ died for the ungodly.

Romans 5:6

When we strive to follow in Jesus's footsteps, we create our own small areas of love, sacrifice, and strength. The road of life was never promised to be a smooth one. There are obstacles and detours, blocks and dead ends. But with faith as our traveling companion, we can make the road a little easier to navigate. If we stay focused on God's direction and love for us, we will arrive at our destination happy and whole.

June 18

We glory in tribulations also: knowing
that tribulation worketh patience.

Romans 5:3

Lord of my heart, give me a refreshing drink from the fountains of your love, walking through this desert as I have. Lord of my heart, spread out before me a new vision of your goodness, locked into this dull routine as I was. Lord of my heart, lift up a shining awareness of your will and purpose, awash in doubts and fears though I be.

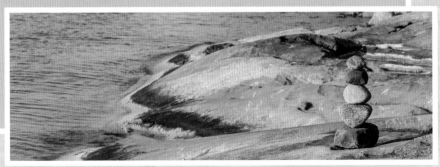

June 19

But God commendeth his love toward us, in that, while we were yet sinners, Christ died for us. Much more then, being now justified by his blood, we shall be saved from wrath through him.

Romans 5:9

To feel love in our hearts, we must first have enough faith to open them wide. The world can be a cold place, but when we approach it with hope and trust in God, we experience such wonders. To be closed off, because of the possibility of pain and suffering, is to never know the feeling of total love of God, of others, and of the good in the world around us.

June 20

For if through the offence of one many be dead, much more the grace of God, and the gift by grace, which is by one man, Jesus Christ, hath abounded unto many.

Romans 5:15

Faith and love go hand in hand, for love itself is an act of extreme faith. Jesus's love and life saved billions — the miraculous power of love. Love is faith in its highest form, acting in the world to spread more happiness, joy and comfort. Love is risky, but only for those without faith to back it up.

June 21

For as by one man's disobedience many were made sinners,
so by the obedience of one shall many be made righteous.

Romans 5:19

*L*ord, remind us that all of creation bears the imprint of your face, all people are children of yours, all souls are illuminated by your divine spark. We know that whatever diminishes others diminishes your spirit at work in them. Make us respectful, humble, and open to the diversity around us that reflects your divine imagination and creativity.

June 22

Therefore as by the offence of one judgment came upon all men to condemnation; even so by the righteousness of one the free gift came upon all men unto justification of life.

Romans 5:18

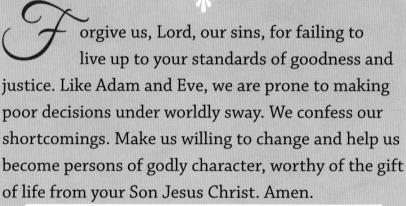

Forgive us, Lord, our sins, for failing to live up to your standards of goodness and justice. Like Adam and Eve, we are prone to making poor decisions under worldly sway. We confess our shortcomings. Make us willing to change and help us become persons of godly character, worthy of the gift of life from your Son Jesus Christ. Amen.

June 23

Many sorrows shall be to the wicked: but he that trusteth in the LORD, mercy shall compass him about.

Psalm 32:10

The support of family and friends is important, but it isn't always consistent. When we want people to believe in us, they sometimes fall short of our expectations. God alone believes in us with unceasing faith and love. So when others are not available for us to lean on, we can always turn to God for the strength and encouragement we need.

June 24

The counsel of the LORD standeth for ever, the thoughts of his heart to all generations.

Psalm 33:11

God, when things go wrong, we usually question you first. Forgive us for wondering if you would deliberately hurt one of your own children. Help us take comfort in your Word as others have done for thousands of years. Thank you for your presence, and please forgive our many sins.

June 25

The LORD bringeth the counsel of the heathen to nought:
he maketh the devices of the people of none effect.

Psalm 33:10

There's a saying that we should forgive and forget, but there are some things I don't think I can forget. I ask in prayer that you help me forgive people of their sins, and let go of them to make way for healing and peace. I no longer want to live in anger and regret, nor do I wish to judge those whom it's up to God alone to assess. Amen.

June 26

But let all those that put their trust in thee rejoice: let them ever shout for joy, because thou defendest them: let them also that love thy name be joyful in thee.

Psalm 5:11

God made friends so that we could be surrounded with angels who love and care for us, who joy in the Lord with us. Always put faith in God first, but have faith in those we love to be there when we cry, when we are happy, and when we need them for guidance. These are God's angels, sent into our lives like an army of blessed beings of light who love us most.

June 27

Have mercy upon me, O LORD; for I am weak:
O LORD, heal me; for my bones are vexed.

Psalm 6:2

When your heart is broken, it's almost impossible to believe you will ever feel whole and loved again. But you will, because the truth is, God is always there for you. Have faith that God will walk with you during the darkest parts of your journey and bring you back into the light stronger and more whole than ever. Have faith in God's love. He will never break your heart.

June 28

Let thy fountain be blessed: and rejoice with the wife of thy youth.

Proverbs 5:18

What is love but the expression of faith towards others? When we love, we do so with the faith that our feelings will be respected, maybe even reciprocated. But even if they aren't, we love anyway, because that is who and what we are. God wants us to have faith in love, and to give of it openly. God wants us to love and be loved in return.

June 29

Say unto wisdom, Thou art my sister; and call understanding thy kinswoman: That they may keep thee from the strange woman, from the stranger which flattereth with her words.

Proverbs 7:4–5

Give me strength today to stand against temptation, Lord, and to recognize those who would lead me toward poor decisions. I know the choice is ultimately my own, but you can help to clear my vision and better guide my heart.

June 30

*Better is a dinner of herbs where love is, than
a stalled ox and hatred therewith.*

Proverbs 15:17

When love knocks, it takes a powerful faith to open the door and welcome it in. I trust that God sends me the right people to help me, care for me, and love me, and that those who present difficulties and challenges are there to teach me great lessons. I let love in, and if I can't enjoy it, I learn from it.

July

July 1

Whoso findeth a wife findeth a good thing, and obtaineth favour of the LORD.

Proverbs 18:22

Though I am alone today, I know God is always with me. I know God always loves me and even if I don't have a partner to share in life's joys and sorrows with, I have God. My faith is in God and his love for me, and that he will one day lead me to a wonderful partner. But if he chooses that I be alone, I will never be lonely with God at my side.

July 2

A man that hath friends must shew himself friendly: and there is a friend that sticketh closer than a brother.

Proverbs 18:24

God has sent us loved ones in the form of human angels, to help us get through the challenges of being alive. These angels may be friends, family or even strangers who appear when we most need them. When we feel alone, we must have faith that angels are all around us ready to help us find our way again.

July 3

Faithful are the wounds of a friend; but the kisses of an enemy are deceitful.

Proverbs 27:6

Thank God for friendship. It brings me joy and comfort and provides refuge from an often harsh world. My friends can share the truth with me and help me to be better, and I, God willing, can do the same for them. Bless me with ears to listen, a shoulder to lean on, and the good sense to build bridges, not walls.

July 4

Ointment and perfume rejoice the heart: so doth the sweetness of a man's friend by hearty counsel.

Proverbs 27:9

We miss so much joy just because we don't open ourselves up to all there is to enjoy. We can choose to embrace all the joy that today has to bring. True joy comes from a celebration of the heart over the things that do not change—things that come from God.

July 5

Teach me thy way, O LORD, and lead me in a plain path, because of mine enemies.

Psalm 27:11

The start of a new relationship, career or a family can bring so much stress and fear. Will it work out? How will I cope if things go wrong? We are filled with doubt and worry when we leave the comfort of what was, to find what can be. But God will be there, walking this new journey with us, holding us up when we stumble. Once we find our faith, we find our footing.

July 6

Wait on the LORD: be of good courage, and he shall strengthen thine heart: wait, I say, on the LORD.

Psalm 27:14

God's faith is in everything we see and touch, everything we feel, and everyone we meet. Patience is one of the virtues we struggle with most, but the sense of "waiting" we feel is also in God's hands. He will deliver.

July 7

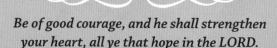

Be of good courage, and he shall strengthen
your heart, all ye that hope in the LORD.

Psalm 31:24

Take comfort in God's steadfast presence. Loving Jesus is not something that happens automatically. It is not something that's easy or natural. It is learned through the trials of life. But as we take on those trials, learn from them, and grow in the Lord, we find strength to take on the next trial.

July 8

Make me to go in the path of thy commandments;
for therein do I delight.

Psalm 119:35

*I*f we could stop pretending to be strong and start being honest with ourselves and God, crying out, "God, please help! I am poor and needy," he would hurry to help us and be the strength of our lives. His rules are clear and simple but they're much harder to faithfully follow. Lucky for us, we can ask for his help to walk in the light of his love and grace.

July 9

Accept, I beseech thee, the freewill offerings of my mouth, O LORD, and teach me thy judgments.

Psalm 119:108

It's amazing what we can accomplish if we keep our eyes off our circumstances and on the One who is in control of them. God, help me to remember to praise you in good times and bad. I can never understand what your plan is for me without your help and guidance.

July 10

The LORD thy God in the midst of thee is mighty; he will save, he will rejoice over thee with joy; he will rest in his love, he will joy over thee with singing.

Zephaniah 3:17

Friends and family members are often separated by distance. But we know that God is the tie that binds us all together, no matter where we are. In our midst, he is as ubiquitous as the air we breathe and the forces of nature that move our world.

July 11

Now therefore, O our God, hear the prayer of thy servant, and his supplications, and cause thy face to shine upon thy sanctuary that is desolate, for the Lord's sake.

Daniel 9:17

Love for God is the best motive for serving. We gather together to serve food to the hungry, give clothes to the needy, or raise emergency funds for hard times in our communities. Even when our sanctuary seems desolate, the ability to serve is in us, and serving our fellow man turns the bright light of God's face toward us.

July 12

To the Lord our God belong mercies and forgivenesses, though we have rebelled against him; Neither have we obeyed the voice of the LORD our God, to walk in his laws, which he set before us by his servants the prophets.

Daniel 9:9–10

Nobody knows someone else's pain, how much she or he hurts, the depth and power of it. Nobody can know for sure except the Lord. And only the Lord can help to relieve this pain, whether physical, spiritual, or emotional.

July 13

And the Lord said unto Abram, after that Lot was separated from him, Lift up now thine eyes, and look from the place where thou art northward, and southward, and eastward, and westward: For all the land which thou seest, to thee will I give it, and to thy seed for ever.

Genesis 13:14–15

God gives because he is love. He gave the world and everything in it. When that was tossed aside, he redeemed mankind with another gift. It was the best he had to offer. The supreme gift. The total gift. In the person of his Son, he gave us himself.

July 14

Hear me when I call, O God of my righteousness: thou hast enlarged me when I was in distress; have mercy upon me, and hear my prayer.

Psalm 4:1

No one likes suffering. But it brings our attention back to God and reminds us how helpless we are without him. Our distress can be mild or severe but our response should always be the same: Lean on God and ask for his help. Like a good Samaritan who holds a door or carries our heaviest bag, God wants to step in to relieve our burden exactly when we need it.

July 15

But know that the LORD hath set apart him that is godly for himself: the LORD will hear when I call unto him.

Psalm 4:3

In the dark night of the soul, a light shines forth, guiding us back to the comfort of solid ground. In the coldest of days, a warmth emerges, giving us new life and hope again. In the loneliest of times, a friend comes forth, one whom we can trust and lean on. God's faith is all of these things, and more.

July 16

There be many that say, Who will shew us any good? LORD, lift thou up the light of thy countenance upon us.

Psalm 4:6

Dear Lord, I pray for a strong spirit to stand against my fears today. I don't ask for fearlessness, because I do feel fear, and I do worry and doubt and I am human. Instead, I pray that you will be at my side in frightening situations, and that you will never leave me abandoned and forgotten. I pray you will shore up my own spirit and give me a sharp mind and deep faith, so that I can overcome any blocks in the road to love, peace and happiness.

July 17

Thou hast put gladness in my heart, more than in the time that their corn and their wine increased.

Psalm 4:7

Instead of feeling overwrought with demands to the point of being overwhelmed, feel the overflowing joy that comes from daily life in the midst of a hustling, bustling family. The two halves make one marvelous whole of God's balance.

July 18

I will both lay me down in peace, and sleep: for thou, LORD, only makest me dwell in safety.

Psalm 4:8

Take comfort in God's steadfast presence. Even when you suffer, take comfort in the hope of God's healing. Even when you fear, take comfort in the hope of God's strength. No matter what you face, take comfort in knowing you never walk alone.

July 19

*Hearken unto the voice of my cry, my King, and
my God: for unto thee will I pray.*

Psalm 5:2

Lord, stand beside me, and hold my hand, but
also give me that extra bit of courage for the
times you ask that I walk through the darkness alone.
Thank you, Lord, for the comfort I find in your Word
and when I speak to you in prayer, knowing that you
hear me and love me. Amen.

July 20

My voice shalt thou hear in the morning, O LORD; in the morning will I direct my prayer unto thee, and will look up.

Psalm 5:3

Dear God, please live in my heart and help me to remain steadfast as I seek to learn, grow, and improve my situation and myself. Please remind me, on the days when my spirit flags, that you are always there. Help me to hear your voice in my heart telling me to take comfort and rest assured in your plan.

July 21

But that no man is justified by the law in the sight of God, it is evident: for, The just shall live by faith.

Galatians 3:11

Be with me now, Lord, as I leave not only a familiar place, but a familiar me. Grant me wisdom to go forward now, toward a new home and life, solitary but free. Be with me as I carry only my faith on this journey; the way home has never seemed longer.

July 22

For this cause also thank we God without ceasing, because, when ye received the word of God which ye heard of us, ye received it not as the word of men, but as it is in truth, the word of God, which effectually worketh also in you that believe.

1 Thessalonians 2:13

Pondering God's goodness fills me with joy. He loves each of us beyond anything we can imagine, a supernatural love that lights our lives and our forevers. His word shows us the potential of faith and good works on earth and in heaven. God is so good!

July 23

As ye know how we exhorted and comforted and charged every one of you, as a father doth his children, That ye would walk worthy of God, who hath called you unto his kingdom and glory.

1 Thessalonians 2:11–12

Young children have a particularly deep capacity for joy. They love fiercely and play hard; their worldview is often one of opportunity and abundance. As we grow, experiences good and bad accrue. We take on more responsibility, for others and for ourselves, and can lose sight of that deep well of joy. God, help us to connect with the powerful joy we find in worshiping you.

July 24

Furthermore then we beseech you, brethren, and exhort you by the Lord Jesus, that as ye have received of us how ye ought to walk and to please God, so ye would abound more and more.

1 Thessalonians 4:1

Lord, we stand in awe of your great sacrifice for us. Your journey to the cross is the reason we are free from the destruction of sin. It's why we can be forgiven and be united with you throughout eternity. No sacrifice is too great in response to your love for us. Keep us ever mindful, Lord. Keep us ever grateful.

July 25

For God hath not called us unto uncleanness, but unto holiness. He therefore that despiseth, despiseth not man, but God, who hath also given unto us his holy Spirit.

1 Thessalonians 4:7–8

God, I pray for your will to be done in my life, and for the fearlessness that comes from having you as my rock and my foundation. I can't let past experiences or grudges hold me back. Let me shine my light, God, and help me not play it safe and miss out on the incredible experiences you have in store for me. Amen.

July 26

And that ye study to be quiet, and to do your own business, and to work with your own hands, as we commanded you; That ye may walk honestly toward them that are without, and that ye may have lack of nothing.

1 Thessalonians 4:11–12

I look around at work and think how wonderful it is that so many different people can become a team. Thank you for the work that keeps me busy and lets me be generous to those less fortunate. Thank you for the friendships I develop with my coworkers and for bringing us together in a special place.

July 27

Prove all things; hold fast that which is good.
Abstain from all appearance of evil.

1 Thessalonians 5:21–22

There is in your grace, God of second chances, insufficient evidence to prove my latest setback is a failure. Even if it is, with you, failure is never final but an opportunity to learn and grow. When I goof, as I am prone to do, help me from doubling the problem by failing to take advantage of your redemption.

July 28

Then we which are alive and remain shall be caught up together with them in the clouds, to meet the Lord in the air: and so shall we ever be with the Lord.

1 Thessalonians 4:17

Joy is the presence of God in our lives, which brings music to our souls. Each day is a veritable walk in the clouds, no matter what befalls us, because God is on our side and waiting to welcome us for eternity. Our safety net is made of clouds.

July 29

Now we exhort you, brethren, warn them that are unruly, comfort the feebleminded, support the weak, be patient toward all men.

1 Thessalonians 5:14

We are called by our creator to care for those around us. We are called to be generous and patient with those who need it most, and to follow Jesus's teachings in this way will buoy us as well. A smile of gratitude or understanding will cure a thousand emotional ills and leave us feeling lighter as we're lifted toward the Lord.

July 30

But as touching brotherly love ye need not that I write unto you: for ye yourselves are taught of God to love one another.

1 Thessalonians 4:9

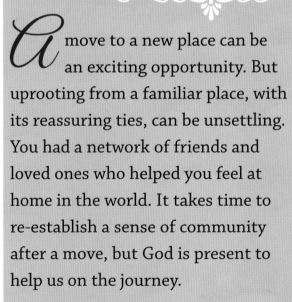 move to a new place can be an exciting opportunity. But uprooting from a familiar place, with its reassuring ties, can be unsettling. You had a network of friends and loved ones who helped you feel at home in the world. It takes time to re-establish a sense of community after a move, but God is present to help us on the journey.

July 31

But let us, who are of the day, be sober, putting on the breastplate of faith and love; and for an helmet, the hope of salvation.

1 Thessalonians 5:8

Jesus's chief desire was to save us from the consequences of our wrong choices and our rejection of God. He paid our debts with his life, and now he's waiting for us to do our part—to turn around and be reconciled to God before the final judgment. Wow! Who has that kind of mercy? Our loving God.

August

August 1

For yourselves know perfectly that the day of the Lord so cometh as a thief in the night. But ye, brethren, are not in darkness, that that day should overtake you as a thief. Ye are all the children of light, and the children of the day: we are not of the night, nor of darkness.

1 Thessalonians 5:2, 4–5

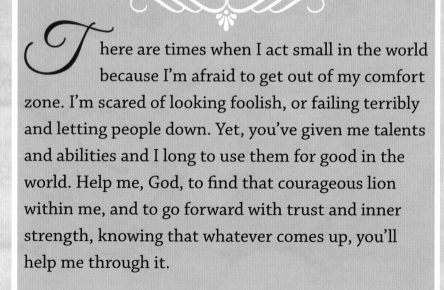

There are times when I act small in the world because I'm afraid to get out of my comfort zone. I'm scared of looking foolish, or failing terribly and letting people down. Yet, you've given me talents and abilities and I long to use them for good in the world. Help me, God, to find that courageous lion within me, and to go forward with trust and inner strength, knowing that whatever comes up, you'll help me through it.

August 2

And the children of Israel, the priests, and the Levites, and the rest of the children of the captivity, kept the dedication of this house of God with joy.

Ezra 6:16

Joy is tricky in that it can manifest itself in opposites: there is joy in community, even as it exists in solitary pursuits. A gorgeous summer sky brings joy, as does a brooding landscape. Sometimes we don't recognize joy, but it is there: we can still access it, whether it feels like good loneliness, hilarity, or a deep stillness. It is a gift we must not lose sight of. Dear Lord, thank you for joy, which comes from you.

August 3

Whatsoever is commanded by the God of heaven, let it be diligently done for the house of the God of heaven.

Ezra 7:23

Heavenly Father, talking to others about you isn't always easy. It's hard for me to express my emotions in mere words. Though I long to tell my children all you mean to me, self-consciousness gets in the way. Help me to speak to them from my heart. Inspire me with language that will fall on fertile soil.

August 4

Remember me, O my God, concerning this, and wipe not out my good deeds that I have done for the house of my God, and for the offices thereof.

Nehemiah 13:14

Lord, I knew the minute the words were out of my mouth that they would have been better left unsaid. Why do I continue to fall into the trap of needing to say what I think at the expense of someone else? Not only did I hurt someone's feelings, but I also looked like a fool in the process! Help me to repair the damage and learn from this experience. Give me another chance to behave nobly by saying nothing.

August 5

Behold, we are servants this day, and for the land that thou gavest unto our fathers to eat the fruit thereof and the good thereof, behold, we are servants in it.

Nehemiah 9:36

Lord, sometimes I think back to who I was before I knew you, and I don't even recognize myself. That's how great the change is when you make us new creations! I'm so glad that the person I was isn't nearly as important in your eyes as the person you know I can be. I may have been younger and fitter then, but I was lost on this worldly adventure. Thank you, Lord, for claiming me as your own and making everything new in my life!

August 6

Nevertheless for thy great mercies' sake thou didst not utterly consume them, nor forsake them; for thou art a gracious and merciful God.

Nehemiah 9:31

When sorrow comes to us, it can be overwhelming. We feel unable to move and incapable of the patience necessary to wait for the healing that will come with time. Knowing you are there, Lord, brings the most comfort. Words fail. Kind gestures fall short. But when we remember that what comforts us most is your mercy, we know what to do: just be there—listening, praying, and loving—allowing your Spirit to pervade the space around us.

August 7

Thou gavest also thy good spirit to instruct them,
and withheldest not thy manna from their mouth,
and gavest them water for their thirst.

Nehemiah 9:20

B less you, our God who cares for us and equips us to go out into the world. The burr under the saddle to go, do, is a gift from you, the Creator who inspires dreams and provides resources to reach them. That's a lesson I'm excitedly learning and I can't wait to share it with others.

August 8

Yet thou in thy manifold mercies forsookest them not in the wilderness: the pillar of the cloud departed not from them by day, to lead them in the way; neither the pillar of fire by night, to shew them light, and the way wherein they should go.

Nehemiah 9:19

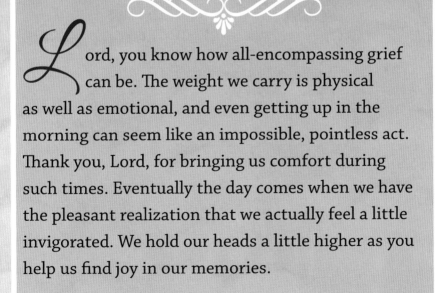

Lord, you know how all-encompassing grief can be. The weight we carry is physical as well as emotional, and even getting up in the morning can seem like an impossible, pointless act. Thank you, Lord, for bringing us comfort during such times. Eventually the day comes when we have the pleasant realization that we actually feel a little invigorated. We hold our heads a little higher as you help us find joy in our memories.

August 9

Iron sharpeneth iron; so a man sharpeneth the countenance of his friend.

Proverbs 27:17

Community enriches us, granting us a sense of belonging, mutual support, and opportunities to exchange ideas and knowledge. We gather together and speak to God in unison, and we use our private conversations with him to better serve our friends and surroundings. Even in an unfamiliar place, have faith that you will find your people.

August 10

The voice of my beloved! behold, he cometh leaping upon the mountains, skipping upon the hills.

Song of Solomon 2:8

Dear Lord, I would love someone special in my life with whom to share my ups and downs and the experiences of being alive. I ask in prayer that you send to me the perfect mate, who is a lover, a friend, a partner and a confidante. I ask for someone I can trust and lean on and laugh with, and someone who shares my views and values, yet challenges me to always think beyond my own limited vision and be more of myself. Lord, direct my steps to this perfect love, one that is perfect for me in your view. Amen.

August 11

Thou art all fair, my love; there is no spot in thee.

Song of Solomon 4:7

As our bodies begin to show signs of age, our inner self is growing in radiance, compounding in beauty, flourishing in faith. We are just beginning to blossom within, just beginning to display a bit of the brightness that will burst forth in heaven when our life is finally fully opened to the light of God's love.

August 12

Set me as a seal upon thine heart, as a seal upon thine arm: for love is strong as death; jealousy is cruel as the grave: the coals thereof are coals of fire, which hath a most vehement flame.

Song of Solomon 8:6

Dear God, guide me along my path, and give me the intuition to make the best decisions for me and for my family. Illuminate my way so that I am not tempted by selfishness or jealousy. Make me not a martyr but a powerful giver. Make me not a victim but a happy participant in all the joys and frustrations of this life I have chosen. Amen.

August 13

Many waters cannot quench love, neither can the floods drown it: if a man would give all the substance of his house for love, it would utterly be contemned.

Song of Solomon 8:7

Make me strong in body and in spirit. Give me a faith that never weakens, and a courage that never wavers. Help me, Lord, to be a rock to those who need me, as you always are to me. Help me to also help myself when no one is around, and to learn to lean on your wisdom and guidance rather than my own. Be my rock and my shield, guarding me from harm. Amen.

August 14

Plead my cause, O LORD, with them that strive with me: fight against them that fight against me.

Psalm 35:1

Sticks and stones of prejudice feel like they're breaking bones. Yet God calls us by name, numbers the hairs on our heads, guards our comings in and goings out, lifts us to high places and sets angels over us. How can we doubt our value with such overwhelming evidence to the contrary!

August 15

Let them shout for joy, and be glad, that favour my righteous cause: yea, let them say continually, Let the LORD be magnified, which hath pleasure in the prosperity of his servant.

Psalm 35:27

With your energetic belief in us, Lord, we know there is no better time than mid-career and mid-life to change course. Middlers have "double vision," seeing both behind and ahead, and the view is exciting. With your help, we see that the glass is more than half full for those who say, "I know where I've been, and the future looks better than the past," and then make a new day happen. Mid-career, mid-life, is as good a time as any to make a change, Lord, and certainly better than never.

August 16

Let them be confounded and put to shame that seek after my soul: let them be turned back and brought to confusion that devise my hurt. Let them be as chaff before the wind: and let the angel of the LORD chase them. Let their way be dark and slippery: and let the angel of the LORD persecute them.

Psalm 35:4–6

The answer to senseless destruction is purposeful creation. Art, in all its forms, is a great healer. If you can write, write. If you can paint, paint. If you're a potter, turn pots. You are a child of God, so fill your life with creation. Channel your pain and spirit into your hands.

August 17

When I said, My foot slippeth; thy mercy, O LORD, held me up.

Psalm 94:18

Miserably, embarrassingly, and very publicly, I made a huge mistake. Peers sympathize but are mostly relieved it was me and not them. Remind me not to gloat the next time I am successful and someone else wears the dunce cap. Be with me as I walk with all eyes on me, chin up, face forward to try again. Help me learn from my failures and remind me that I am not a failure.

August 18

They break in pieces thy people, O LORD, and afflict thine heritage.
They slay the widow and the stranger, and murder the fatherless.
Yet they say, The LORD shall not see, neither shall the God of Jacob
regard it. Understand, ye brutish among the people: and ye fools,
when will ye be wise? He that planted the ear, shall he not hear? he
that formed the eye, shall he not see?

Psalm 94:5–9

How can I live in a place like this? Where people keep fighting over status and power, where most of the words are unkind at best, where grasping is the main activity, lying an everyday thing? Where the smiling face, the helping hand, seem jarring in their out-of-placeness? How could you travel and preach in a place like that, Jesus? How did you do it?

August 19

Unless the LORD had been my help,
my soul had almost dwelt in silence.

Psalm 94:17

Our families suffer, too, O God, as illness runs its course. Faces show strain from trying not to worry; voices sound too bright from unshed tears. Strengthen them for the grueling task that awaits; their support is life-sustaining.

August 20

God hath from the beginning chosen you to salvation through sanctification of the Spirit and belief of the truth.

2 Thessalonians 2:13

Oh, Lord, I feel your presence:
Love and warmth and light.
My troubled soul is open,
And soon my heart feels right.

I bask for just a moment,
In the light of love he gives.
I'm filled with God's assurance,
That YES, my Savior lives.

August 21

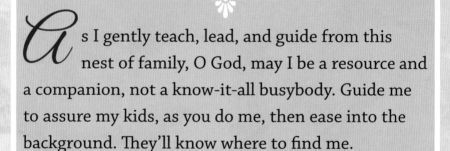

Therefore, brethren, stand fast, and hold the traditions which ye have been taught, whether by word, or our epistle.

2 Thessalonians 2:15

As I gently teach, lead, and guide from this nest of family, O God, may I be a resource and a companion, not a know-it-all busybody. Guide me to assure my kids, as you do me, then ease into the background. They'll know where to find me.

August 22

Now our Lord Jesus Christ himself, and God, even our Father, which hath loved us, and hath given us everlasting consolation and good hope through grace, Comfort your hearts, and stablish you in every good word and work.

2 Thessalonians 2:16–17

More than boards and mortar, O God our shelter, this home stands on you as the foundation, giving all who live here a refuge not only for the body but also for the mind and the soul.

August 23

Neither did we eat any man's bread for nought; but wrought with labour and travail night and day, that we might not be chargeable to any of you.

2 Thessalonians 3:8

Lord, is this really what work is meant to be? Can you make it sing again? Put the spark back in my zeal? Because I know that work is a blessed privilege; I don't want to be ungrateful. But how boring the piles of paperwork, how deadening the countless reports, how fatiguing the endless round of meetings. Yes, I need to feel it again, Lord—the joy. Help!

August 24

*For we hear that there are some which walk among you disorderly,
working not at all, but are busybodies. Now them that are such
we command and exhort by our Lord Jesus Christ, that
with quietness they work, and eat their own bread.*

2 Thessalonians 3:11–12

From infancy, it's hard not to choose for your child. It's a riddle, O God, why you give us freedom to choose. Didn't you know it could break a mother's heart? Comfort me as I cope with a choice not mine; forgive any role I had in it. Keep me from saying, "I told you so."

August 25

O God, thou art my God; early will I seek thee: my soul thirsteth for thee, my flesh longeth for thee in a dry and thirsty land, where no water is; To see thy power and thy glory, so as I have seen thee in the sanctuary.

Psalm 63:1–2

God of doves and rainbows, we know what hope looks like as family, advocates, friends, and those who've shared similar fates accompany us through this dark tunnel of crisis. Behind these faces, we recognize yours.

August 26

Because thy lovingkindness is better than life, my lips shall
praise thee. Thus will I bless thee while I live: I will
lift up my hands in thy name.

Psalm 63:3–4

Lord, empower me with the vitality to keep up with these kids. Embolden me with courage to face each day's pressing problems. Enlighten me with creative ways to juggle the responsibilities in front of me. Enrich my inner world so that when my outer world goes crazy, I don't go crazy along with it! Embrace me when I am too tired, too scared, and too insecure to make even the smallest decision. Entertain me when they've all gone off to work and school and I am home alone again. Thank you, Amen.

August 27

Hear my prayer, O LORD, and let my cry come unto thee. Hide not thy face from me in the day when I am in trouble; incline thine ear unto me: in the day when I call answer me speedily.

Psalm 102:1–2

Here they go, O God, my no-longer-babies. Out of my arms and into their world. Steady me as I pause at each threshold. I dare only follow at a distance lest they see me hovering and think they can't do it alone. Or, worse, that I can't. Help me find ways to show I know we both can.

August 28

My days are like a shadow that declineth; and I am withered like grass. But thou, O LORD, shall endure for ever; and thy remembrance unto all generations.

Psalm 101:11–12

The Light of Love I yearn for
Needs only my request
I close my eyes and ask God
For calm and quiet rest.

A stillness soon takes over,
Loosening the bind.
Serenity and God's peace
Have cleared my troubled mind.

August 29

Giving thanks unto the Father, which hath made us meet to be partakers of the inheritance of the saints in light: Who hath delivered us from the power of darkness, and hath translated us into the kingdom of his dear Son.

Psalm 15:1

Your Word has said we are to be imitators of you, to live in love, to be forgiving and tenderhearted. I have tried to be kind and loving in all circumstances, but I have not always succeeded. Yet in your tender mercy, you have allowed some of your goodness to shine through in my family and the rest of my life. I am so grateful.

August 30

For by him were all things created, that are in heaven, and that are in earth, visible and invisible, whether they be thrones, or dominions, or principalities, or powers: all things were created by him, and for him: And he is before all things, and by him all things consist.

Psalm 15:1

As I follow in the children's wake as they discover bugs, plants, and cloud faces, your awesome creations bring us to our knees in daily thankfulness as we learn to name and know the works of your hands, Loving Creator.

August 31

And you, that were sometime alienated and enemies in your mind by wicked works, yet now hath he reconciled in the body of his flesh through death, to present you holy and unblameable and unreproveable in his sight.

Colossians 1:21–22

Precious Lord, fostering kindness in children isn't easy because they are so centered on their own wants and needs. But Lord, I praise you for signs of kindness I have seen in my children. As they grow, I see more evidence of their reaching out to others, and I am thankful. Continue to develop in their hearts a compassion for the poor, the ill, the unfortunate, the outcast, so each day they may grow more like you.

September

September 1

That their hearts might be comforted, being knit together in love, and unto all riches of the full assurance of understanding, to the acknowledgement of the mystery of God, and of the Father, and of Christ; In whom are hid all the treasures of wisdom and knowledge.

Colossians 2:2–3

God bless this joyful life I have been given. God bless my family and my home. God bless my friends and neighbors and the people I meet along the way. God bless the joy and the pain, the pleasure and the frustration. God bless every moment of it!

September 2

Beware lest any man spoil you through philosophy and vain deceit, after the tradition of men, after the rudiments of the world, and not after Christ.

Colossians 2:8

Things get broken, plans changed. And in God's grace, mothers are good at contingency plans. So are kids. Their spirits are inherently shining and optimistic. Making something useless into useful is a lesson they grasp. They love nothing better than cutting, pasting, and gluing back together. Their joy and gratitude shows on their sweet faces.

September 3

Let no man therefore judge you in meat, or in drink, or in respect of an holyday, or of the new moon, or of the sabbath days: Which are a shadow of things to come; but the body is of Christ.

Colossians 2:16–17

Pay cuts and wage freezes have come as a shock, Lord, and I'm working harder for less. My worldly life is second to my eternal life but I still must pay my bills. Help me learn to balance not just the checkbook but my consumer appetites as well, so I can remember what's really important, in both lean and fat times.

September 4

Let no man beguile you of your reward in a voluntary humility and worshipping of angels, intruding into those things which he hath not seen, vainly puffed up by his fleshly mind.

Colossians 2:18

God, I am scurrying around like a chicken with its head cut off, making a huge mess everywhere I go. Why, God, when I know I do better and work more efficiently when I wait quietly and listen for your guidance, do I rush about—driven by time rather than by you? Help me, God, to slow down, to be silent, so I can hear you and do your will, not mine.

September 5

Set your affection on things above, not on things on the earth. For ye are dead, and your life is hid with Christ in God.

Colossians 3:2–3

Keep us connected, O God of all time, to those who've come before. Inspire us to tell family tales and to pull out family albums and family Bibles and handed-down antiques to show the connecting links of which your love forges us into a whole. Our loved ones sit beside you and make ripples through the generations.

September 6

But now ye also put off all these; anger, wrath, malice,
blasphemy, filthy communication out of your mouth.

Colossians 3:8

laying favorites can be destructive.
Joseph's brothers were torn apart by their
father's partiality to him. King Saul was driven mad
by the favoritism the public showed David. You treat
all people alike, Lord. We are all your children. Please
help me to do the same, and guard me from even the
appearance of favoritism in my life. Thank you for
making each one of us feel like your favorite.

September 7

And let the peace of God rule in your hearts, to the which also ye are called in one body; and be ye thankful.

Colossians 3:15

Help me see the connection between our relationship, O God, and the ones I have with others: my spouse, my friends, but especially the children. I use them all as excuses for not praying when they're a prime reason to pray! Hear me now.

September 8

Let the word of Christ dwell in you richly in all wisdom; teaching and admonishing one another in psalms and hymns and spiritual songs, singing with grace in your hearts to the Lord.

Colossians 3:16

Help me listen between the beats of my headache to hear hearts overflowing with enthusiasm and joy. Join our parade, God of music and motion; it's simple, but it's in your honor. Let us all make a "noiseful" joy.

September 9

And whatsoever ye do, do it heartily, as to the Lord, and not unto men; Knowing that of the Lord ye shall receive the reward of the inheritance: for ye serve the Lord Christ.

Colossians 3:23–24

Lord, let me be sensitive to the subtle messages my children are receiving regarding their self-worth. Help me to show my confidence in each child and to remind them all that they matter to our family. They also matter to you, Lord, for you are the God who cares for and values each of your children. Give my young ones the assurance that comes with knowing they are the children of a King.

September 10

Masters, give unto your servants that which is just and equal; knowing that ye also have a Master in heaven.

Colossians 4:1

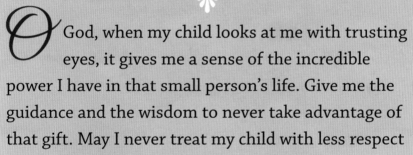

O God, when my child looks at me with trusting eyes, it gives me a sense of the incredible power I have in that small person's life. Give me the guidance and the wisdom to never take advantage of that gift. May I never treat my child with less respect than I would treat myself. And grant that if I do falter and use this special life for my own gain, that you would humble me with the realization that parenting is not about cloning but about creating unique persons.

September 11

Walk in wisdom toward them that are without, redeeming the time.

Colossians 4:5

While terror rages, we cling together by candlelight, drawing courage from one another until the dawn comes again. In the meantime, we walk together in the Lord and share our fears in hopes of finding our strength. It is then that God will bring us a happier day.

September 12

Let your speech be always with grace, seasoned with salt,
that ye may know how ye ought to answer every man.

Colossians 4:6

Death is not an end to be dreaded for those who love the Lord. This fact is difficult for us to "live out" in our daily lives, but we can better seize our days by learning to be the best and most godly versions of ourselves. Others are more likely to emulate Christians who are role models of kindness and generosity without seeming aloof or judgmental.

September 13

Now therefore thus saith the LORD of hosts; Consider your ways.

Haggai 1:5

*L*ord, I've learned how to pray in strange but necessary places: in carpools, while cooking dinner, at the dentist, between loads of laundry, waiting in the checkout line. I've discovered that it's not how long I pray that matters but rather the very act of attempting to make a connection with you.

September 14

Judge me, O God, and plead my cause against an ungodly nation: O deliver me from the deceitful and unjust man.

Psalm 43:1

Why am I so uneasy?
What's this quest I make?
The mystery is fleeting;
This longing's hard to shake.

I'm told there is a warm light
Filled with hope and love,
A light that fills our souls up,
A glow sent from above.

September 15

O send out thy light and thy truth: let them lead me; let them bring me unto thy holy hill, and to thy tabernacles.

Psalm 43:3

Help us to relax, Lord of calm and peace, so that we don't become numb to the joy and awe of your beautiful world. It's socially acceptable to kick off our shoes and tangibly feel your love through the soft green grass. Make us alive, O God, to the holy grounds of life, and save us from taking these special places for granted.

September 16

Dear Lord, my love for you is heartfelt: I feel it in my heart. Every day you surprise me with gifts, new challenges, and twist endings to the many story threads that make up each life. The best part is the friends and family I've found who feel the same way about you. At any special moment, I know someone will catch my eye and say, "God is so good."

September 17

I am Alpha and Omega, the beginning and the ending, saith the Lord, which is, and which was, and which is to come, the Almighty.

Revelation 1:8

When you feel swept along, remember that God has a plan for you. His might and power are in everything you ever touch, every prayer you send his way, and every choice you make. If your relationship with God is solid, you can never stray far from the right path.

September 18

He that hath an ear, let him hear what the Spirit saith unto the churches; To him that overcometh will I give to eat of the tree of life, which is in the midst of the paradise of God.

Revelation 2:7

Thank you, God, for my life. Today I realize I have so much to be thankful for. My life may not be perfect, but nevertheless it is full of good things, of beauty, and of many wonders. Thank you, Lord, for everything you have given me and the opportunities I've had. Please make me aware of all I have to celebrate and be thankful for.

September 19

I know thy works, and charity, and service, and faith, and thy patience, and thy works; and the last to be more than the first.

Revelation 2:19

O Lord, if you don't remember our sins, why do we so often beat ourselves up over them? The only possible benefit I can see is that this way, there's less chance that we'll repeat them. But if it be your will, Lord—and to our benefit—grant us your sweet forgetfulness. We accept your gift of forgiveness, Lord. May we learn to accept your gift of forgetfulness as well.

September 20

As many as I love, I rebuke and chasten:
be zealous therefore, and repent.

Revelation 3:19

Once a verbal barb is out there, there's no taking it back. It may have felt good for a moment, but the sense of triumph gives way almost immediately to a sense of regret. If wisdom rules our tongues, however, the sword of our words will defend and encourage those around us. It will secure honor and blessing by its careful use and make those around us feel secure rather than threatened.

September 21

Behold, I stand at the door, and knock: if any man hear my voice, and open the door, I will come in to him, and will sup with him, and he with me.

Revelation 3:20

It's simple: Listen for God. Listen with all your senses, your heart, your mind, and your gut instinct. And if you can't hear him, find a more quiet place. Calm your anxieties and fears, step away for a few minutes, and sit in complete silence with your thoughts. Welcome God's voice into your house.

September 22

*Thou art worthy, O Lord, to receive glory and honour and
power: for thou hast created all things, and for
thy pleasure they are and were created.*

Revelation 4:11

God, we praise you in gratitude for the world
we live in, the families we're blessed with,
and the opportunities we have every day. Through
your power we're able to live happy, healthy lives on
earth as messengers and to spend eternity with you.
Words can't express how thankful we are.

September 23

For the great day of his wrath is come; and
who shall be able to stand?

Revelation 6:17

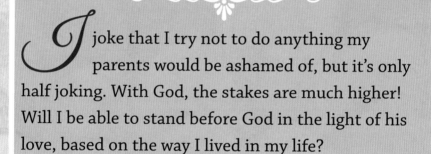

I joke that I try not to do anything my parents would be ashamed of, but it's only half joking. With God, the stakes are much higher! Will I be able to stand before God in the light of his love, based on the way I lived in my life?

September 24

Our soul is escaped as a bird out of the snare of the fowlers: the snare is broken, and we are escaped. Our help is in the name of the LORD, who made heaven and earth.

Psalm 124:7–8

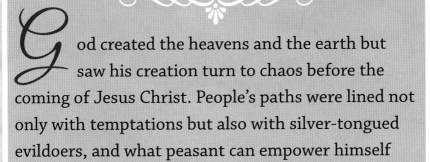

God created the heavens and the earth but saw his creation turn to chaos before the coming of Jesus Christ. People's paths were lined not only with temptations but also with silver-tongued evildoers, and what peasant can empower himself to stand up to a corrupt king? God appeared again and again to show the right way and empower the people.

September 25

As the mountains are round about Jerusalem, so the LORD is round about his people from henceforth even for ever.

Psalm 125:2

Lord, allow me to be the kind of parent that my child can be proud of. I try to protect my kids as I also teach them to make their own choices. It's tempting to control too much of their lives out of a misguided sense of my own better judgment, but your teachings don't support that and I know in my heart that it's not the right way. Help me to surround my kids with protective love but not smother them. Amen.

September 26

*Do good, O LORD, unto those that be good, and
to them that are upright in their hearts*

Psalm 125:4

There are times when doing the right things, and "being good," doesn't seem to reward us enough. No one seems to care that we went out of our way to turn in a lost briefcase. Our so-called enemies don't notice how much we love them. Forgiveness, in real life, often leads to ambivalent, tough standstills in our relationships as we figure things out. But God is watching and he always knows.

September 27

For thus saith the LORD, Ye shall not see wind, neither shall ye see rain; yet that valley shall be filled with water, that ye may drink, both ye, and your cattle, and your beasts.

2 Kings 3:17

God always provides. It can be frustrating that we don't see his machinations at work, which leads to puzzling times as we think about a sign or feeling we received or an outcome that doesn't seem to help us. But we know he always provides.

September 28

And he said, Come with me, and see my zeal for the LORD.

2 Kings 10:16

Who guides and protects me in my life? Today, I am grateful for the people who have brought me to where I am today and who always have my best interests at heart. I may not always have appreciated their guidance, but I know deep down they always meant well. In the same way, Lord, let me accept and appreciate your guidance in my life.

September 29

But the LORD your God ye shall fear; and he shall
deliver you out of the hand of all your enemies.

2 Kings 17:39

Let God be the wind in your sail that carries
you to safety from the dark chaos of a storm.
All you need to do is prostrate yourself and ask.

September 30

And Hezekiah prayed before the LORD, and said, O LORD God of Israel, which dwellest between the cherubims, thou art the God, even thou alone, of all the kingdoms of the earth; thou hast made heaven and earth. LORD, bow down thine ear, and hear: open, LORD, thine eyes, and see.

2 Kings 19:15–16

My cluttered mind needs clearing;
Tangled thoughts are tied.
I relax, breathe deep, and wait
For His presence by my side.

October

October 1

Now therefore, O LORD our God, I beseech thee, save thou us out of his hand, that all the kingdoms of the earth may know that thou art the LORD God, even thou only.

2 Kings 19:19

Sit with me, God of broken dreams, in the debris of my family. Toddler tantrums, teen rebellion, young-adult resistance. Prop me up to make peace for another day and to show a thoughtful, Christian example to my children and those around us. I'm humbled by your awesome, heavy gift of parenthood.

October 2

I beseech thee, O LORD, remember now how I have walked before thee in truth and with a perfect heart, and have done that which is good in thy sight.

2 Kings 20:3

*L*ord, I've never had a perfect heart, but I've done my best to walk your path. How inspiring and energizing to know you love me for who I am and still offer me the gift of eternal life. I need only ask.

October 3

It is of the LORD's mercies that we are not consumed, because his compassions fail not. They are new every morning: great is thy faithfulness.

Lamentations 3:23

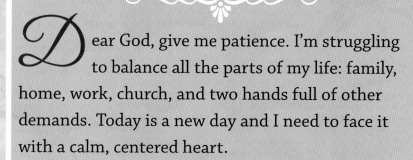

Dear God, give me patience. I'm struggling to balance all the parts of my life: family, home, work, church, and two hands full of other demands. Today is a new day and I need to face it with a calm, centered heart.

October 4

The LORD is my portion, saith my soul; therefore will I hope in him.

Lamentations 3:24

Wing and harp and robe of white
Sliding through the day and night
Spirit beings bathed in light
We walk by faith, not by sight

October 5

The LORD is good unto them that wait for him,
to the soul that seeketh him.

Lamentations 3:25

God, allow me to be the kind of guardian that will protect my child from harm. As I rely on you to keep me safe, fortify me to keep my child safe. Shore me up to be strong even when I feel tired and weak, to be patient when I am harried and exhausted. Help me to follow your example.

October 6

*It is good that a man should both hope and quietly
wait for the salvation of the LORD.*

Lamentations 3:26

We are given the gift of freedom, the freedom to risk, to make mistakes, and even to fail. We live with the twin pillars of God's plan for us and our own freedom to choose. We ask for God's help while we also know he provides for us. These behaviors may seem at odds to those who don't have faith.

October 7

Let us search and try our ways, and turn again to the LORD.

Lamentations 3:40

I pray for a stronger, deeper faith in the perfection of my life, even if I can't make sense of it right now. I pray for more spiritual endurance and fortitude when I feel like giving up. I pray for the strength to examine myself and reach for God for help.

October 8

Let us lift up our heart with our hands unto God in the heavens.

Lamentations 3:41

Before I became a parent, I didn't think much about how children imagine God. Through simple graces to bless childhood fare and bedtime prayers to offer you the day, I'm honored to introduce you to my child now. But how can I explain who you are to such a little one as this?

October 9

I called upon thy name, O LORD, out of the low dungeon.
Lamentations 3:55

Headlines tell a dark sorry tale, God, and depress us about money problems, strife, drugs, and school problems; about housing, wildlife, family, and health problems. These problems will also inevitably touch our lives. Thank you for waiting to hold our hand at our lowest points and darkest moments and lead us up toward the light again. Amen.

October 10

*Thou hast heard my voice: hide not thine ear
at my breathing, at my cry*

Lamentations 3:56

May you be healed, in mind, body, and soul. May you come to know that all healing proceeds from God, and he cares about every part of you. Perhaps the healing will come sooner for your attitude than for your body. Perhaps your mind will experience peace quicker than bones and muscles. But sooner or later, all will be well.

October 11

Thou drewest near in the day that I called upon thee: thou saidst, Fear not.

Lamentations 3:57

Lord, today I am nervous, but I take comfort in your resilience. I may make silly mistakes, blundering through facts that I know as well as my own name. However, Lord, with you at my elbow, I may just as likely be at ease, competent, and pleasant. Either way, I know I'll survive. No matter today's outcome, remind me to look in the mirror you hold up so that I can see a reflection of someone who did their best.

October 12

God is our refuge and strength, a very present help in trouble. Therefore will not we fear, though the earth be removed, and though the mountains be carried into the midst of the sea; Though the waters thereof roar and be troubled, though the mountains shake with the swelling thereof.

Psalm 46:1–3

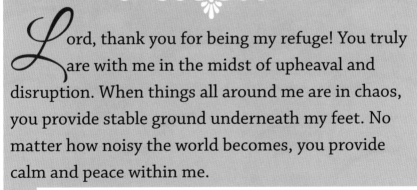

Lord, thank you for being my refuge! You truly are with me in the midst of upheaval and disruption. When things all around me are in chaos, you provide stable ground underneath my feet. No matter how noisy the world becomes, you provide calm and peace within me.

October 13

O LORD, thou hast pleaded the causes of my soul; thou hast redeemed my life.

Lamentations 3:58

May the gifts and talents God has given become apparent to you. And with that recognition, may there also arise a clear sense of where to apply them. A career is an important thing. For God's will is your fulfillment; your being in just the right place is the joy of his heart.

October 14

*So foolish was I, and ignorant: I was as a beast before
thee. Nevertheless I am continually with thee:
thou hast holden me by my right hand.*

Psalm 73:22–23

In the raising of children, Lord, can I teach
what I can't do? To observe them is to know
that they're already developing skills they see me
model. O God, help! To
equip them to become the
best they can be, I must
start with myself. Guide
me to do my best. Amen.

October 15

Thou shalt guide me with thy counsel, and
afterward receive me to glory.

Psalm 73:24

In these modern times, we often come together as pieces of a puzzle that can't quite fit together without help. Bless and lead us, a new family in the making, God of unity. Turn us around, sort us out, and reassemble us in a satisfying whole.

October 16

*Whom have I in heaven but thee? and there is
none upon earth that I desire beside thee.*

Psalm 73:25

Only God's love can truly satisfy my soul. All other forms of love are in God's honor—we strive to live by his values and build sacred homes and communities for ourselves. We emulate his love for us in our love for our fellow man.

October 17

My flesh and my heart faileth: but God is the strength of my heart, and my portion for ever.

Psalm 73:26

Illness requires new math, O God, subtraction of old fears and addition of new thought. Help me bring this lesson home as I draw ten stick figures, color the percentage said to recover from this ailment, and write my name on the brightest figure! A most deserving child, I praise you for the resources to make it happen. Sharing with you divides my troubles and multiplies my healing chances.

October 18

If we say that we have no sin, we deceive ourselves, and the truth is not in us. If we confess our sins, he is faithful and just to forgive us our sins, and to cleanse us from all unrighteousness. If we say that we have not sinned, we make him a liar, and his word is not in us.

1 John 1:8–10

The truth can be difficult to face, but if we are always desiring to seek and face the truth, our lives will be much richer. Being willing to dig deeper for truth is a sign of godliness.

October 19

But whoso keepeth his word, in him verily is the love of God perfected: hereby know we that we are in him. He that saith he abideth in him ought himself also so to walk, even as he walked.

1 John 2:5–6

When we step out and do the thing we believe God wants us to do, even if it doesn't make sense, that's faith. Our greatest rewards can come from those acts.

October 20

This then is the message which we have heard of him, and declare unto you, that God is light, and in him is no darkness at all. If we say that we have fellowship with him, and walk in darkness, we lie, and do not the truth: But if we walk in the light, as he is in the light, we have fellowship one with another, and the blood of Jesus Christ his Son cleanseth us from all sin.

1 John 1:5–7

*P*erseverance is possible as long as we remain convinced that God is at work—changing people, adapting our circumstances, and cleansing us of our sins.

October 21

Love not the world, neither the things that are in the world. If any man love the world, the love of the Father is not in him. For all that is in the world, the lust of the flesh, and the lust of the eyes, and the pride of life, is not of the Father, but is of the world. And the world passeth away, and the lust thereof: but he that doeth the will of God abideth for ever.

1 John 2:15–17

God, you're leading me. With confidence I face my day. Every duty and interruption are appointments you've sent my way. I bide my time in this world for you in the next.

October 22

For this is the message that ye heard from the beginning, that we should love one another.

1 John 3:11

Bless my family, O God, for it is unique . . . some say too much so. I am grateful you know we are joined by love—for each other and for and from you. We are grateful you use more than one pattern to create a good family. This pioneering family has you at its heart. Our love is what glues us together.

October 23

Marvel not, my brethren, if the world hate you.

1 John 3:13

Strengthen our resolve, O God, to take better care of our worldly selves, for we eat, drink, and choose risky lifestyles and then want to blame you! As we live with our consequences, help us know you as the loving parent who weeps first when your children get themselves into trouble. Remind us that we're only passing through this world.

October 24

My little children, let us not love in word,
neither in tongue; but in deed and in truth.

1 John 3:18

God does not love us so that we can hoard his love for ourselves. He desires that we pass it on to others. By spreading the joy of his love, we improve the lives of those around us—and our own lives in the process.

October 25

And hereby we know that we are of the truth, and shall assure our hearts before him. For if our heart condemn us, God is greater than our heart, and knoweth all things.

1 John 3:19–20

Defeat has stopped me in my tracks. I see no options, no possibilities. Yet paralyzing doubt can be relieved by finding something to believe in, something as simple as dandelions, rainbows, dawn, thunder and lightning. God will find me there. He sees the big picture and his plans for me even when I can't see anything for myself.

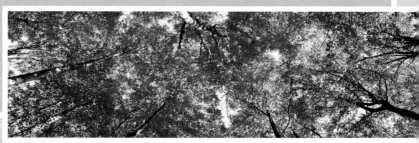

October 26

And whatsoever we ask, we receive of him, because we keep his commandments, and do those things that are pleasing in his sight. And this is his commandment, That we should believe on the name of his Son Jesus Christ, and love one another, as he gave us commandment.

1 John 3:22–23

When it seems that scarcely a day ends by saying, "If only I could do it over. I regret what I said, did, or didn't do," the God of fresh starts is eager to make things right. All you need to say is, "Forgive me for today, and show me how to redeem myself for tomorrow." Faith will deliver you.

October 27

I will seek that which was lost, and bring again that which was driven away, and will bind up that which was broken, and will strengthen that which was sick.

Ezekiel 34:16

O God, healing is going so-o-o-o slowly, and I am impatient and grumpy. Mind, body, or soul, this could take a long time. Remind me that recovery is a journey, not a hasty jet-lagged arrival. Bless me with faith to sustain me, step by small step. You do miraculous things with faith as tiny as mustard seeds that, in time, blossom into awesome growth. I hold that picture as I make mustard-seed progress along the road to healing.

October 28

And I will make with them a covenant of peace, and will cause the evil beasts to cease out of the land: and they shall dwell safely in the wilderness, and sleep in the woods. And I will make them and the places round about my hill a blessing; and I will cause the shower to come down in his season; there shall be showers of blessing.

Ezekiel 34:25–26

When we draw a circle around ourselves to shut him out, God draws a larger circle to take us in. He builds a shelter around us and envelops us in safety and love.

October 29

Thus shall they know that I the LORD their God am with them, and that they, even the house of Israel, are my people, saith the Lord GOD. And ye my flock, the flock of my pasture, are men, and I am your God, saith the Lord GOD.

Ezekiel 34:30–31

It's humbling—and exciting—to know that God sees us worthy of setting a standard for our children by offering options and being strong enough to maintain them. He cares for us as a shepherd for his flock, and we care for our own flocks in his image.

October 30

I waited patiently for the LORD; and he inclined unto me, and heard my cry. He brought me up also out of an horrible pit, out of the miry clay, and set my feet upon a rock, and established my goings. And he hath put a new song in my mouth, even praise unto our God: many shall see it, and fear, and shall trust in the LORD.

Psalm 40:1–3

I can't count the days since I last prayed much less considered God's ideas about what I'm doing. I've been "too busy" . . . until I realized I was losing my cool with regularity and acting entirely too big for my shoes!

October 31

Many, O LORD my God, are thy wonderful works which thou hast done, and thy thoughts which are to us-ward: they cannot be reckoned up in order unto thee: if I would declare and speak of them, they are more than can be numbered.

Psalm 40:5

*H*elp me count your blessings, Lord, although I can never reach the end. Your number line stretches into the horizon and beyond, giving me new reasons to be thankful each and every day. Amen.

November

November 1

Then said I, Lo, I come: in the volume of the book it is written of me, I delight to do thy will, O my God: yea, thy law is within my heart.

Psalm 40:7–8

Send the sun's light through creation: surf and skyline merging, bird song and flight. Send it through people: friends who laugh at our jokes, family who never stray. Send it through inner knowing: unexplained peace and joy, faith that you're working alongside us. Lord, we celebrate your truth and stretch tall with gladness in the sunshine.

November 2

I have not hid thy righteousness within my heart; I have declared thy faithfulness and thy salvation: I have not concealed thy lovingkindness and thy truth from the great congregation. Withhold not thou thy tender mercies from me, O LORD: let thy lovingkindness and thy truth continually preserve me.

Psalm 40:10–11

Keep me calm, Lord, during this hard time. Changes and challenges tear me down me like a tornado through town and I'm left reeling. I'm tempted to finish the job with harsh words and other self-destructive actions. In the dust cloud I've created, I need sunshine to bring your love back to me.

November 3

For innumerable evils have compassed me about: mine iniquities have taken hold upon me, so that I am not able to look up; they are more than the hairs of mine head: therefore my heart faileth me. Be pleased, O LORD, to deliver me: O LORD, make haste to help me.

Psalm 40:12–13

As fickle as the weather, growing children change moods, clothes, and values, disrupting the family in the process. In the struggle to grow up and away, they go too far, and we are left in the wake like a torn tail on a kite. God's is the shoulder to lean on while we catch our breath.

November 4

Let all those that seek thee rejoice and be glad in thee: let such as love thy salvation say continually, The LORD be magnified. But I am poor and needy; yet the Lord thinketh upon me: thou art my help and my deliverer; make no tarrying, O my God.

Psalm 40:16–17

Dreams are another form of hope; and hope is God opening a door. God's awesome power allow him to help everyone who asks for it, but our different situations mean we may feel like he isn't working fast enough for us. We must be patient.

November 5

Blessed be God, even the Father of our Lord Jesus Christ, the Father of mercies, and the God of all comfort; Who comforteth us in all our tribulation, that we may be able to comfort them which are in any trouble, by the comfort wherewith we ourselves are comforted of God. For as the sufferings of Christ abound in us, so our consolation also aboundeth by Christ.

2 Corinthians 1:3–5

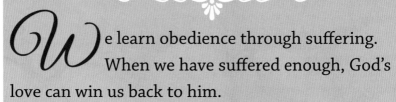

We learn obedience through suffering. When we have suffered enough, God's love can win us back to him.

November 6

And our hope of you is stedfast, knowing, that as ye are partakers of the sufferings, so shall ye be also of the consolation.

2 Corinthians 1:7

We are born with no shame and with the innocence of an infant. But when life slows us down, we sometimes believe that we are unworthy of love. God reminds us that he loves us and that our obstacles and roadblocks are only speed bumps before the better things ahead.

November 7

*Now the Lord is that Spirit: and where the
Spirit of the Lord is, there is liberty.*

2 Corinthians 3:17

Dear God, give us the courage to "unplug" on evenings or Sundays to replenish and enjoy the simple pleasures of one another's company. Keep us focused on your promised restfulness instead of on the world's distractions, at least for a while.

November 8

But have renounced the hidden things of dishonesty, not walking in craftiness, nor handling the word of God deceitfully; but by manifestation of the truth commending ourselves to every man's conscience in the sight of God.

2 Corinthians 4:2

From the beginning of our lives we are taught to walk, speak, to run, to love, to receive, and to give in return. For our moral lives we are taught to tell the truth, be charitable, and so much more. We are taught by people who know us well and those who don't know us at all. And we are taught by God's word.

November 9

For we preach not ourselves, but Christ Jesus the Lord; and ourselves your servants for Jesus' sake. For God, who commanded the light to shine out of darkness, hath shined in our hearts, to give the light of the knowledge of the glory of God in the face of Jesus Christ.

2 Corinthians 4:5–6

We are big on heroes, God. Every area of our lives has a favorite except perhaps the most important: our faith. An Aquinas or Augustine can't hold a candle to the Hollywood celebrities of our day. How sad we willingly settle for superficiality rather than substance. Jesus was a "rock star" in his time; let's make him that famous again today.

November 10

We are troubled on every side, yet not distressed; we are perplexed,
but not in despair; Persecuted, but not forsaken; cast down, but not
destroyed; Always bearing about in the body the dying of the Lord
Jesus, that the life also of Jesus might be made manifest in our body.

2 Corinthians 4:8–10

Thank you, God, that I'm not the same person today as I was even just a few years ago. This new life as a parent writes its changing tale on my heart, face, and mind like growth rings on a tree. So much of your Word rings true to me now in a way I never understood before. The highest highs and lowest lows come in pairs and are made bearable by your love.

November 11

But though our outward man perish, yet the inward man is renewed day by day.

2 Corinthians 4:16

*L*ike potpourri, the unique individual "ingredients" of a family make a wondrous mixture, stirred as it is by God's enduring hand of possibilities.

November 12

For our light affliction, which is but for a moment, worketh for us a far more exceeding and eternal weight of glory.

2 Corinthians 4:17

I chase after symptoms like a child playing tag. Stay with me on good days and bad and the precarious ones in between; I feel so alone, separate as I feel even from my own body. You are the only constant in my life, promising the eternal reward.

November 13

While we look not at the things which are seen, but at the things which are not seen: for the things which are seen are temporal; but the things which are not seen are eternal.

2 Corinthians 4:18

May you enjoy a new job. Slide into it with a calm heart. Don't become overwhelmed with all your new responsibilities. God can help you approach each task, one at a time, starting on your very first day. Look to him, and your new friends, for all you need. The job is of the world but the fellowship may be so much more!

November 14

Praise the LORD from the earth, ye dragons, and all deeps: Fire, and hail; snow, and vapours; stormy wind fulfilling his word: Mountains, and all hills; fruitful trees, and all cedars: Beasts, and all cattle; creeping things, and flying fowl: Kings of the earth, and all people; princes, and all judges of the earth: Both young men, and maidens; old men, and children: Let them praise the name of the LORD: for his name alone is excellent; his glory is above the earth and heaven.

Psalm 148:7–13

When life's taken its best shot, dig in and lift eyes skyward. Feel it? That's God's spirit and immortal power blowing across weary lives, filling us with a second wind.

November 15

Praise ye the LORD. Praise ye the LORD from the heavens: praise him in the heights. Praise ye him, all his angels: praise ye him, all his hosts. Praise ye him, sun and moon: praise him, all ye stars of light. Praise him, ye heavens of heavens, and ye waters that be above the heavens.

Psalm 148:1–4

So often, Patient One, we become stifled, leading to boredom and whining when circumstances are not as we would have them. What power there is in seeking things not as they are but as they might be, O God, as the children—and I—learn invaluable truths as close as our own backyard. We give thanks and praise for your limitless creation.

November 16

Let them praise the name of the LORD: for he commanded, and they were created. He hath also stablished them for ever and ever: he hath made a decree which shall not pass.

Psalm 148:5–6

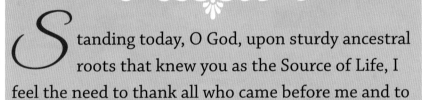

Standing today, O God, upon sturdy ancestral roots that knew you as the Source of Life, I feel the need to thank all who came before me and to drop to my knees in gratitude to you. We are safe and sheltered in your love forever and ever, through all the generations.

November 17

Behold, the LORD thy God hath set the land before thee: go up and possess it, as the LORD God of thy fathers hath said unto thee; fear not, neither be discouraged.

Deuteronomy 1:21

*L*ife's not fair, and I stomp my foot in frustration. The powerful get more so as the rest of us shrink, dreams for peace are shattered as bullies get the upper hand, and despair is a tempting pit to fall into. Help me hold on, for you are a God of justice and dreams, of turning life upside down. Let me help; thanks for listening in the meantime.

November 18

Ye shall not fear them: for the LORD your God he shall fight for you.

Deuteronomy 3:22

The armor of God will shield us from dangers we haven't even thought of yet. Accept doubts that come about work, about family, about the future—whatever—for they are magnifying glasses that clarify thoughts, beliefs, and dreams and strengthen resolve that in God's hands becomes more than enough.

November 19

Only take heed to thyself, and keep thy soul diligently, lest thou forget the things which thine eyes have seen, and lest they depart from thy heart all the days of thy life: but teach them thy sons, and thy sons' sons.

Deuteronomy 4:9

God, I hold my children close to me the way you keep me close with you. Please help me to teach them. Allow me to be the kind of friend that my child will turn to. Allow me to be the kind of mentor that my child will seek advice from. Allow me to be the kind of parent that my child would one day like to be. Amen.

November 20

Go thou near, and hear all that the LORD our God shall say: and speak thou unto us all that the LORD our God shall speak unto thee; and we will hear it, and do it.

Deuteronomy 5:27

Trying to find relief on "those days," it's so easy to forget that the world's way of TV, computer games, shopping, snacking, and other guilty pleasures are no substitute for God's companionship and guidance. Earthly comforts are okay as long as we don't confuse them with the truly meaningful influence of God's light in our lives.

November 21

Ye shall walk in all the ways which the LORD your God hath commanded you, that ye may live, and that it may be well with you, and that ye may prolong your days in the land which ye shall possess

Deuteronomy 5:33

Angels walk by your side every day in every place, keeping you on God's path. They love us no matter what happens. They are sent to us as an extension of God's hand. God reaches his hand to you through angels you have never seen as well as people you've seldom been without.

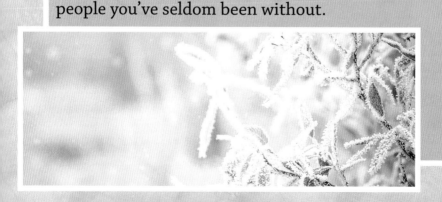

November 22

And thou shalt love the LORD thy God with all thine heart, and with all thy soul, and with all thy might.

Deuteronomy 6:5

Loving God, I have dedicated my children to you and have promised to teach them your laws. May this tree of life continue to grow into the future where I will provide limbs of love from which my children can launch their own lives. Sometimes I feel ineloquent, inadequate, unfit for the task. But you are with me, Lord; you can supply what I lack.

November 23

Thou shalt fear the LORD thy God, and serve him, and shalt swear by his name.

Deuteronomy 6:13

Backyard adventures, like discovering the migrating butterflies that stopped to rest in the trees, draw us into accepting our role as caretaker of God's marvelous creation, a daily reminder of God's presence in our lives. We devote our lives to Him with gladness and gratitude in our hearts.

November 24

God is our refuge and strength, a very present help in trouble.

Psalm 46:1

Creator of the earth, you are the God of sun and sky, trees and grass, fruit and flowers—the God of growing things. I offer my praise and gratitude for the quiet loveliness of my garden, where I can delight in the constant renewal of life. Help me to remember that though I plant and water, it is you who provides the life and growth—the therapeutic retreat.

November 25

Will not we fear, though the earth be removed, and though the mountains be carried into the midst of the sea; Though the waters thereof roar and be troubled, though the mountains shake with the swelling thereof.

Psalm 46:2–3

When I am lonely and afraid you
whisper, "Child, fear not."
When I simply can't go on you
say, "Take one more shot."
When nothing seems to go my
way you tell me, "Trust . . . you'll see!"
Like an angel on my shoulder,
God, you're always there for me.

November 26

There is a river, the streams whereof shall make glad the city of God, the holy place of the tabernacles of the most High. God is in the midst of her; she shall not be moved: God shall help her, and that right early.

Psalm 46:4–5

Gracious God, help me to reflect your warmth to my family, to reflect your light that sparks their imagination and kindles their compassion. May my children know your presence through me, through the way I embody your spirit to them. Help me to change the world by creating children who exude warmth and light, dispelling the shadows around them.

November 27

My brethren, count it all joy when ye fall into divers temptations;
Knowing this, that the trying of your faith worketh patience.

James 1:2—3

Father, you are the God of peace. Fill me with your quiet spirit. Teach me to get control of my anger before lashing out at the children. Prevent me from blaming them instead of calmly stating the reasons for my anger. Remind me that my aim is to soothe not to stir up anger. Give me a tongue that is soft and gentle rather than harsh and perverse so my young ones will be inspired to change their behavior.

November 28

If any of you lack wisdom, let him ask of God, that giveth to all men liberally, and upbraideth not; and it shall be given him.

James 1:5

Talk about being torn, O Merciful God. I am when it comes to this correcting business. I know giving loving guidance can be life-enhancing, but, if done improperly, it can rob others of their individuality. Give me guidance to know when I am acting creatively and lovingly and when I am overstepping my place. Then, correct me, O Forgiving God.

November 29

For the sun is no sooner risen with a burning heat, but it withereth the grass, and the flower thereof falleth, and the grace of the fashion of it perisheth: so also shall the rich man fade away in his ways.

James 1:11

How can we convince our loved ones that *things* can't make them happy? How do we instill in them the values that will make their lives fulfilling? Help us, O Lord, to plant in their hearts yearnings for the important things in life, such as friendships, love for God, healthy bodies, creative minds, and helping hearts.

November 30

Blessed is the man that endureth temptation: for when he is tried, he shall receive the crown of life, which the Lord hath promised to them that love him.

James 1:12

We try to live modestly and not flaunt our belongings before those who have less. But our children are surrounded by playmates who pile up possessions only to tire of them and quickly discard them. Our children are envious and think they, too, need the latest toys and the trendiest clothes. Our children are our most valued treasures. Humbly we commend them to your care.

December

December 1

Every good gift and every perfect gift is from above, and cometh down from the Father of lights, with whom is no variableness, neither shadow of turning.

James 1:17

Thank you, O God, for those moments of indescribable joy that surprise, that greet me unexpectedly in a hug, a drawing, a conversation, an uncontrollable giggle, and most especially an openness that not only lets me into my family's lives but draws me in.

December 2

Wherefore, my beloved brethren, let every man be swift to hear, slow to speak, slow to wrath: For the wrath of man worketh not the righteousness of God.

James 1:19–20

Guide me, O God, to savor today and all that is yet to be discovered. I know that what came before and what is yet to be form a marvelous mosaic of the whole. Guide me to heal any hurt feelings, saddened hearts, and lonely days so that I leave the world a better place tonight than it was this morning.

December 3

For if there come unto your assembly a man with a gold ring, in goodly apparel, and there come in also a poor man in vile raiment; And ye have respect to him that weareth the gay clothing, and say unto him, Sit thou here in a good place; and say to the poor, Stand thou there, or sit here under my footstool: Are ye not then partial in yourselves, and are become judges of evil thoughts?

James 2:2–4

Studies show again and again how we group together by all our "tribes": social class, race, culture, and more. God, only you can truly judge. Please help me to catch my own profound failures of judgment, hopefully before I do any damage. Everyone deserves a fair and equal chance.

December 4

What doth it profit, my brethren, though a man say he hath faith, and have not works? can faith save him? If a brother or sister be naked, and destitute of daily food, And one of you say unto them, Depart in peace, be ye warmed and filled; notwithstanding ye give them not those things which are needful to the body; what doth it profit?

James 2:14–16

Dear God, show us ways we can help your hurting, needful world. Our children need to see that we are not helpless or hopeless but that all efforts, small as they might seem, can matter. Your world could use our creative kind of mothering.

December 5

Faith, if it hath not works, is dead, being alone. Yea, a man may say, Thou hast faith, and I have works: shew me thy faith without thy works, and I will shew thee my faith by my works.

James 2:17–18

God, please help me find the time. Time to work on my own life, time to follow my own dreams, time to listen to the prompting of my own inner voice. As the days grow shorter outside, let me make use of my time in the highest and best ways. Guide me to channel your spirit into the works I feel passionate about.

December 6

For every kind of beasts, and of birds, and of serpents, and of things in the sea, is tamed, and hath been tamed of mankind: But the tongue can no man tame; it is an unruly evil, full of deadly poison.

James 3:7–8

Loving God, sometimes when my children and I have a difference of opinion, they translate that difference as a lack of care for them. Everything I do is for them. How can I convince them that I am on their side—that my opposition to their opinions or actions grows out of my love and concern for them?

December 7

Therewith bless we God, even the Father; and therewith curse we men, which are made after the similitude of God. Out of the same mouth proceedeth blessing and cursing. My brethren, these things ought not so to be. Doth a fountain send forth at the same place sweet water and bitter? Can the fig tree, my brethren, bear olive berries? either a vine, figs? so can no fountain both yield salt water and fresh

James 3:9–12

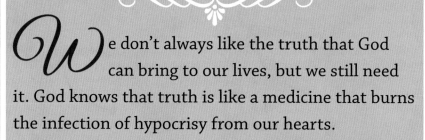

We don't always like the truth that God can bring to our lives, but we still need it. God knows that truth is like a medicine that burns the infection of hypocrisy from our hearts.

December 8

But the wisdom that is from above is first pure, then peaceable, gentle, and easy to be intreated, full of mercy and good fruits, without partiality, and without hypocrisy.

James 3:17

Being an adviser to these offspring is both exhausting and exhilarating. At times I even think myself wise, until they reject my sageness as old-fashioned. Remind me, O God of wisdom, that they are not so much rejecting my knowledge as they are entering their own new, unchartered territory. Make me wise enough to advise them that they have what it takes to enjoy the journey without me having to highlight the route for them.

December 9

Submit yourselves therefore to God. Resist the devil, and he will flee from you. Draw nigh to God, and he will draw nigh to you. Cleanse your hands, ye sinners; and purify your hearts, ye double minded.

James 4:7–8

It's amazing, steadfast God, how much better I feel after sharing with you even the smallest doubt or little niggling worry about being the best person I can be. Connected, we can do great things. Alone, I am the victim of my own fears.

December 10

Humble yourselves in the sight of the Lord, and he shall lift you up.
James 4:10

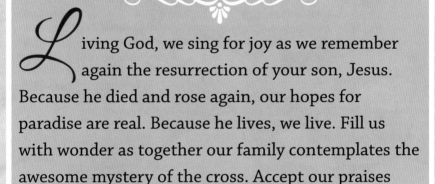

Living God, we sing for joy as we remember again the resurrection of your son, Jesus. Because he died and rose again, our hopes for paradise are real. Because he lives, we live. Fill us with wonder as together our family contemplates the awesome mystery of the cross. Accept our praises and our songs of gratitude. Alleluia!

December 11

Speak not evil one of another, brethren. He that speaketh evil of his brother, and judgeth his brother, speaketh evil of the law, and judgeth the law: but if thou judge the law, thou art not a doer of the law, but a judge. There is one lawgiver, who is able to save and to destroy: who art thou that judgest another?

James 4:11–12

God tells us repeatedly that we must not judge one another, because we have no high ground compared with His infinite wisdom. And in very pragmatic terms, there is no room in a friendship or relationship for one who judges, condemns, and blames. We will all take our turn as the one needing forgiveness and compassion.

December 12

Whereas ye know not what shall be on the morrow. For what is your life? It is even a vapour, that appeareth for a little time, and then vanisheth away.

James 4:14

Father God, protect me from the pull of projects that claim too much of my time. It's so hard to say "no." You know me, Lord. You know what is best for me. You know what I can do and what I must do. Help me to choose wisely the activities that will be of most benefit to my whole family during this fleeting time on earth.

December 13

Be patient therefore, brethren, unto the coming of the Lord. Behold, the husbandman waiteth for the precious fruit of the earth, and hath long patience for it, until he receive the early and latter rain.

James 5:7

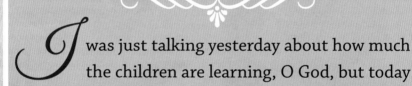

I was just talking yesterday about how much the children are learning, O God, but today I realize that I, too, am continuing to grow and learn. May I never stop being a patient "student" of your will as I move through this wondrous passage of mothering.

December 14

*Grudge not one against another, brethren, lest ye be condemned:
behold, the judge standeth before the door.*

James 5:9

God, give me strength. Please give
me strength!
When my little girl breaks my favorite
crystal bud vase,
And my son gets permanent marker
on his hands and face,
And I find old candy wrappers
all over the place,
God, give me strength!

December 15

Behold, we count them happy which endure. Ye have heard of the patience of Job, and have seen the end of the Lord; that the Lord is very pitiful, and of tender mercy.

James 5:11

It's late at night, and still there is much to do. Yet there is peace, holding on to a child-like trust that God is an ever-present companion, showing us how not to worry needlessly, burning the candle at both ends.

December 16

And the prayer of faith shall save the sick, and the Lord shall raise him up; and if he have committed sins, they shall be forgiven him.

James 5:15

Father, guide me daily. You are a God of infinite kindness and patience. Let the waves of your love wash over me. When rough times occur, enable me to keep others' behaviors in perspective, and let me look at their undesirable actions through eyes filtered by your love. Help me deal with them in an effective way, one that is acceptable to you.

December 17

Confess your faults one to another, and pray one for another, that ye may be healed. The effectual fervent prayer of a righteous man availeth much.

James 5:16

Walk with us and guide us as we encourage our children to be truthful. Keep the lines of communication open between us so they won't feel the need for falsehood. When a lapse occurs, put forgiveness in our hearts so we can put the incident behind us and help our children walk in truth once more.

December 18

Brethren, if any of you do err from the truth, and one convert him; Let him know, that he which converteth the sinner from the error of his way shall save a soul from death, and shall hide a multitude of sins.

James 5:19–20

As the children encounter the rough places of life, Lord, may I find wisdom to help them turn it into something better. Just as an oyster uses a grain of sand to make something better, please continue to inspire us, O God, to find the positive in every situation.

December 19

I long to show my loved ones how to walk daily in your light, to bask in your warmth, and to love you with all of their hearts. Please grant me the understanding I need to show each child how to worship and obey you, so they may experience the joy of your presence in their lives. Your love fills me with song, O Lord. Help me teach the words to my children.

December 20

Know ye that the LORD he is God: it is he that hath made us, and not we ourselves; we are his people, and the sheep of his pasture.

Psalm 100:3

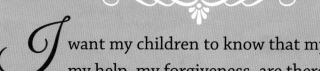

I want my children to know that my love, my help, my forgiveness, are there for the taking; that I am always ready to listen to and comfort them. Lord, your great love has at times been misunderstood and misinterpreted by your children. You have been down this same road. Help me to demonstrate that I care. Let my love penetrate the walls that go up between me and my children, just as your love has done when I've turned away from you.

December 21

Enter into his gates with thanksgiving, and into his courts with praise: be thankful unto him, and bless his name.

Psalm 100:4

There is a choice, O God, when I spot the crayon markings on the wall, the spilled food, the wet towel on the bed. I have equal breath to scream or laugh. I feel the insistent tickle of my funny bone, and I know which choice you will. Thank you for the great blessing of humor.

December 22

For the LORD is good; his mercy is everlasting; and his truth endureth to all generations.

Psalm 100:5

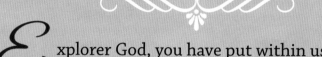

Explorer God, you have put within us a spirit of joy and wonder to move us beyond the immediate and to explore even our most familiar environment to its fullest potential. May each day become an adventure of people, tasks, places, and responsibilities. And when I feel gray and lifeless, may your Spirit remind me that each day brings its own gifts and that the best is yet to be.

December 23

But I will sacrifice unto thee with the voice of thanksgiving; I will pay that that I have vowed. Salvation is of the LORD.

Jonah 2:9

Trying to find relief on during the busy and stressful holidays, it's so easy to forget that the world's way of TV, computer games, shopping, snacking, and other guilty pleasures is no substitute for God's companionship and guidance. Help me to put spiritual capital in the bank even when I feel stretched too thin. Amen.

December 24

When my soul fainted within me I remembered the LORD:
and my prayer came in unto thee, into thine holy temple.

Jonah 2:7

Progress, in the folds of a family, O God, is not a straight, flat line but rather ups and downs. Like squiggles on a heart monitor, they merely chart the daily rhythm of life. Give me energy and patience to go with the flow.

December 25

Behold, a virgin shall be with child, and shall bring forth a son, and they shall call his name Emmanuel.

Matthew 1:23

*L*ord, you are truly with us, today and every day. On this Christmas day, let me be astonished anew at the miracle of your birth and your presence with us today. Let me look with fresh eyes at the age-old story and regard it with a child's wonder, celebrating with the angels in saying, "Glory to God in the highest."

December 26

But let man and beast be covered with sackcloth, and cry mightily unto God: yea, let them turn every one from his evil way, and from the violence that is in their hands.

Jonah 3:8

A walk in the yard bears treasures, like fallen twigs and branches. Yet our children so quickly turn them into swords, and those innocent moments can turn into genuine disputes and hurt feelings. Take away our love of violence, our way of creating weapons from peaceable moments. Help us desire being grounded as well as entertained.

December 27

Out of the depths have I cried unto thee, O LORD. Lord, hear my voice: let thine ears be attentive to the voice of my supplications.

Psalm 130:1–2

ord, you are the God of all that is good. Help me to be firm yet fair when these situations occur. Surround my children with your love, and open their eyes to your truth. Insulate them from the pressures that would weaken our family's witness to the world.

December 28

If thou, LORD, shouldest mark iniquities, O Lord, who shall stand?
But there is forgiveness with thee, that thou mayest be feared

Psalm 130:3–4

In my attempts to "get it right" as I order my life and the lives of those in my family, remind me, O Creator God, to look around and see how you have brought order to our world. Such balance, such harmony, such stability. May I find the faith to trust you like a bird trusts the winds that allow it to soar. Forgive me for my attempts at waxen wings.

December 29

I wait for the LORD, my soul doth wait, and in his word do I hope.
Psalm 130:5

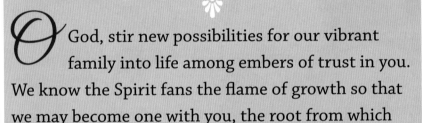

O God, stir new possibilities for our vibrant family into life among embers of trust in you. We know the Spirit fans the flame of growth so that we may become one with you, the root from which we, leaf and folk, have their source.

December 30

My soul waiteth for the Lord more than they that watch for the morning: I say, more than they that watch for the morning.

Psalm 130:6

O God, when I'm tempted to answer questions the children haven't even asked or give simple answers when they need to discover something on their own, gently shush my mouth and still my thoughts. I am to guide, not to do everything. Help me wait and be patient.

December 31

Repent, and be baptized every one of you in the name of Jesus Christ for the remission of sins, and ye shall receive the gift of the Holy Ghost. For the promise is unto you, and to your children, and to all that are afar off, even as many as the Lord our God shall call.

Acts 1:38–39

Sometimes, God, I get too persnickety and alarmingly bossy. I suppose I think it's a way I can reassert control of my life. When that happens, shake me up like a snow globe so I can be real. Truly, messily, and welcomingly real—ready for redemption and joy.